NEWCOMER'S HANDBOOK®

FOR Boston

2nd Edition

FIRST BOOKS

P.O. Box 578147
Chicago, IL 60657
(773) 276-5911
www.firstbooks.com

Authors: Marietta Hitzemann and Ed Golden
Publisher and Editor: Jeremy Solomon
Assistant Editor: Sharon Lanza
Cover design: Miles DeCoster
Interior design and production: Erin Johnson
Maps: Scott Lockheed

ISBN 0-912301-40-6

Manufactured in the United States of America.

Published by First Books, Inc., 6750 SW Franklin, Portland, OR, 97223, 503-968-6777.

CONTENTS

CONTENTS *(continued)*

Welcome to Boston, the "Athens of America," the Hub, the home of the bean and the cod — and academia. You're going to love it here; most newcomers do. You can gorge on cheap seafood, experiment with ethnic foods that you never knew existed, spend days searching through galleries looking for the perfect phrenology head, live in a national historic district, sleep where Washington slept, bike or in-line skate for miles through the heart of the city along the Charles River, listen to the Boston Pops for free at the Hatch Memorial Shell, or spend the rest of your life testing coffee shops and book stores. But first, you'll have to get settled in. The first thing you may want to do is buy a good map and begin to explore. Rest assured, the transition will definitely be worth it!

Depending on where you choose to live, you might not need a car. Thirty-nine percent of Boston's households report their members do not own a car, yet they manage to get around quite easily. Boston's efficient public transportation system makes life without a vehicle convenient and hassle-free. Actually, owning a car during a Boston winter can be a dreary experience. Boston was built for 17th and 18th century traffic, and its old-est streets are simultaneously picturesque and narrow. Parking availibility may be an important factor in your search for a new apartment or home.

As you will soon notice, this guide covers more than the city of Boston proper. Boston hasn't annexed any of the area's many separate towns and cities, most of which are just as old as Boston. Each of the surrounding communities has a distinct history and personality which complements and adds to Boston's diversity. The City of Boston proper has a population of approximately 500,000 people. It's the greater Boston area that adds up: almost five million. One of these surrounding communities may just be the right place for you. Or, you may decide to live in one of Boston's many colorful neighborhoods. Wherever you settle, it is important to know your neighborhood: establishing a sense of community where you will live will make your life in Boston more rewarding.

In addition to regular updating and detailed descriptions of neighborhoods in the city and beyond, this second edition of the *Newcomer's Handbook® for Boston* includes chapters on **Child Care and Education**. The chapter on **Helpful Services** surveys resources and services for people with disabilities as well as new information on keeping a pet in Boston.

As usual, we welcome reader suggestions and comments on the tear-out page at the back of the book.

We hope that the information presented on the following pages will help you establish a Boston residence smoothly and speedily. We also hope that once you select your neighborhood and settle in, the book will help you get on with the pleasure part: enjoyment of the city's myriad resources.

Boston's neighborhoods offer history, diversity, community, and recreation. With more than 40 colleges and universities in metro-Boston, the population on the whole is young. Although Boston area residents do define themselves by the neighborhood or community in which they live, they also venture into other neighborhoods. Boston's energetic medley of streets ensures that no matter where you live, you'll find yourself heading to the Theater District for a dance concert or play, to Chinatown for dim sum on Sunday morning, to the North End for pastry and cappuccino, to Brookline for bagels, and to Harvard Square for people-watching.

Boston is no different than the rest of the country in that crime is a fact of life. Your search for your first home in the Boston area will include making a decision about what you feel comfortable with — though that may change as you get used to your new city. One of the best ways to protect yourself is to pick a neighborhood with a strong sense of community. This is easy to do in Boston where community organizations and ties flourish. Also, look for senior citizens, young families or people who work out of their home on your prospective street. People who are home all day can keep an eye on the neighborhood.

Be aware that parking in Boston is always tight and winter makes it worse. Residents often mark parking spots with trash cans and chairs once they've shoveled their way out. Obviously the streets are public and you can park where you want. Nevertheless, when it snows, Bostonians can get territorial about their parking spaces.

The neighborhood profiles in this *Newcomer's Handbook®* begin with central Boston and Charlestown, then move to western and southern neighborhoods. The surrounding communities follow, roughly counter-clockwise beginning in the north with Cambridge. Each neighborhood profile includes some vital statistics (post office, library branch, police station, etc.) and a description of where newcomers will feel the most comfortable. Following these profiles, you'll find apartment finding suggestions, information about basic services, and places to visit for recreation and entertainment.

Boston Neighborhoods
Beacon Hill/West End
NorthEnd/Waterfront
Charlestown
Back Bay
South End
Allston-Brighton
Jamaica Plain
Roslindale
West Roxbury
East Boston
Dorchester

Surrounding Communities
Cambridge
Somerville
Arlington
Belmont
Watertown
Waltham
Newton
Brookline
Medford
Quincy
Other neighborhoods and additional areas

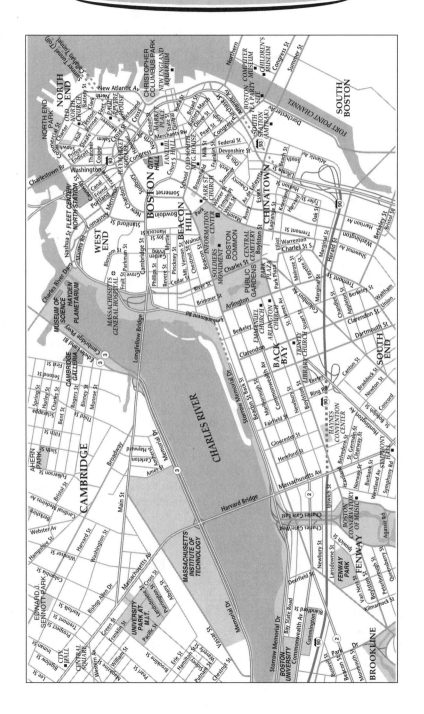

BOSTON

BEACON HILL/WEST END

Boundaries: *Beacon Hill.* **North:** Cambridge Street. **East:** Somerset Street. **South:** Boston Common. **West:** Arlington Street and the Charles River. *West End.* **North:** Nashua Street. **East:** Stanford Causeway. **South:** Cambridge Street. **West:** the Charles River.

Beacon Hill, named after a sentry light set up to warn settlers of possible invasion, is where the Reverend William Blaxton, Boston's first settler, made his home in 1625. Thousands of people live here today, sharing the hill with a state government housed in the gold-domed state capitol designed by architect Charles Bullfinch.

Beacon Hill is a National Historic District and the architecture is early to mid-19th century. Red brick rowhouses with hidden gardens and bay windows, elm-lined cobblestone streets and sidewalks and authentic gas-lit street lanterns make this area the most photographed of all of Boston's neighborhoods. Residents here feel a sense of civic pride in their neighborhood, pride encouraged through window box competitions and annual public tours of the hidden gardens.

Retaining this colonial look requires a certain amount of discipline and regulation. The Beacon Hill Architectural Commission rules on what colors are historically appropriate for window boxes and front doors. Modern amenities, other than cars, must be hidden. For example, air conditioners are not allowed in front windows. "Air space" is regulated as well: getting a permit to build a deck can take years. Beacon Hill's residents understand that their colonial look takes some effort and are used to working with the system. One resident descibes the neighborhood as "cozy and bustling." It also offers spectacular views of the Charles River and sections of Boston.

This area has always been home to some of Boston's wealthiest residents, and it shares with Back Bay the honor of having the highest property values and rents in the city. However, it isn't an exclusively wealthy neighborhood. The Hill's residents refer to an informal division between the "North Slope" or the "back side" and the "South Slope" or the "state house side," with Pinckney Street as the dividing line. The South Slope, which houses the old money folk, was pasture and grass until the late 18th century. The North Slope is home to many graduate students and young professionals. The population here is diverse in age and profession.

Although Beacon Hill retains an old world look, it definitely has new world amenities. With six lanes, Cambridge Street is nothing if not modern, housing a Stop and Shop supermarket, a triple screen cinema, neighborhood bars and ethnic restaurants. Many neighborhood services (dry cleaning, hardware, delis, drug stores) can also be found in the old world shopping district on Charles Street. The **Charles River** serves as Beacon Hill's back yard while the **Boston Common** and the **Public Garden** are its front yard.

The Hill's 18th-century cobblestone streets are quaint but they are so narrow that the neighborhood's parking situation is dismal. Due to the lack of space, very little off-street parking is available. The city issues more residents-only parking stickers than there are parking spaces which means residents here often spend a lot of time circling the neighborhood looking for parking.

The Boston Common Parking Garage, a public garage located on Charles Street across from the Public Garden, helps to alleviate parking shortages in both Beacon Hill and the east side of Back Bay. Parking is available to vehicles less than 6 feet 3 inches in height. Rates are $4/hour for the first two hours between 6 a.m. to 6 p.m. during the week. Parking for up to 12 hours costs $11, and 24 hours will run you $19. Weekends are $6 overnight and $6 Saturday and Sunday days. For more info call: 954-2096.

However, this location (so close to downtown, Chinatown and the Financial District) means that you rarely need your car anyway, unless, of course, you're traveling out of town.

Beacon Hill and the **West End** are separate areas and, to some extent, separate neighborhoods. However, as the majority of rentals in the West End are in the Cambridge Street area and along Charles Street/Storrow Drive, and the Cambridge Street boundary is rather blurry, we've included the West End in this description.

The West End is the informal birthplace of Boston's historic preservation movement. During modernization projects in the 1950s and early 1960s most of the West End — as well as Scollay Square now known as Government Center — was razed and rebuilt. Once modernization was underway the area served as sort of an urban lesson and Boston's preservation societies began to form in order to stop the process from accelerating elsewhere.

The West End is home to both Mass General Hospital and Mass Eye and Ear. There are a number of upscale high-rise apartment buildings along Storrow Drive. The Charles River Park complex is the most famous because of the billboards in front of it taunting the commuter traffic along Storrow Drive/Charles Street with the slogan "if you lived here you'd be home by now."

Area Code: 617

Zip Codes: Beacon Hill: 02108, 02114. West End: 02114

Post Offices: Charles Street Branch, 136 Charles Street, 723-1951; JFK Branch, New Chardon Street, 523-3145; State House Branch, in the State House, 742-7277.

Police District: District A1, Area A, 40 New Sudbury Street, 343-4627 (Community Affairs Office).

Emergency Hospital: Mass General Hospital, 32 Fruit Street, 724-4123.

Libraries: West End Branch, 151 Cambridge Street, 523-3957; Kirstein Business Branch, 20 City Hall Avenue, 523-0860.

Public School Education: North Zone: Blackstone Elementary, 380 Shawmut Avenue, 635-8471; Farragut Elementary, 10 Fenwood Road, 635-8450; Hurley Elementary, 70 Worcester Street, 635-8439; Quincy Elementary, 885 Washington Street, 635-8497; William Carter School, 396 Northampton Street, 635-9832; Boston Latin, 78 Avenue Louis Pasteur, 635-8895; Snowden International High, 150 Newbury Street, 635-9989.

Public Transportation: access to all subways or trolleys via Park Street Station, Government Center and Downtown Crossing.

NORTH END/WATERFRONT

Boundaries: *North End:* **North and East:** Commercial Street. **South and West:** Central Artery. *Waterfront:* **North and East:** Boston Harbor. **South:** Fosters Wharf. **West:** Commercial Street and Atlantic Avenue.

The North End is Boston's Little Italy. As the city's oldest residential section, the North End is historically important for its architecture and street layout. The streets haven't changed since colonial days, and Hanover Street has been the major north-west corridor since 1660. Today the North End houses a multigenerational Italian-American community with deep traditions, colorful street festivals, strong ethnic pride and excellent restaurants and cafes. However, many non-Italian-Americans live in the North End and their number is increasing. The area is well-known for seafood, espresso and 24 hour-a-day bakeries. You can find fresh pasta, gelati, espresso, authentic Italian pizza, pastry, fresh produce and fresh fish on the streets of the North End.

During pre-Revolutionary days, the North End was the fashionable district of Boston where colonial governors built their mansions. However as many of the North End's inhabitants were Loyalist British supporters, these leading merchants and residents were forced to abandon their properties and flee after the colonies won the Revolutionary War.

Waves of immigrants moved in and out of the North End during the nineteenth and early twentieth centuries. An Irish influx made up the major group moving into the North End during the 1820s, changing to Jewish newcomers from Eastern Europe by the 1860s. In turn, they were replaced by the Portuguese and then by the Italians.

The neighborhood is densely populated with tightly built-up streets. Small inner courts are abundant. The narrow, twisting cobblestone streets are jam-packed with shops and cafes. If you are looking for wide open spaces rather than a cozy neighborhood, the North End is not for you. A female North End resident reports: "I live alone but I never feel lonely." The neighborhood has a crowded, Old World look and feel due in part to its predominant masonry apartment blocks with ground level shops that date from the early eighteenth century.

The North End is an affordable, safe option but parking is with resident stickers only and there isn't enough of it to go around.

Believe it or not, this tightly packed community does offer some open space. North End green space includes Copp's Hill Burying Ground (established 1659), Copp's Hill Terraces (established 1896-97), Paul Revere Mall ("the Prado") and Christopher Columbus Park (also known as Waterfront Park).

The boundary between the North End and the **Waterfront** is quite fluid. Many people consider the Waterfront a part of the North End. However, North End housing is more reasonably priced than the Waterfront's.

The Waterfront was nearly abandoned in the early 1900s but began a rebirth in the 1960s. Local architects started renovating old wharf buildings, turning them into condos and apartments. This area is now Boston's newest "mixed use" (commercial, residential, etc.) district and is also a desirable address (i.e. pricey). The residents in the Waterfront's condos and apartments are pretty upscale but a few less well-to-do artists live in the Fort Point Channel Lofts.

Boston's waterfront is one of the most accessible of any major American city. The finger piers maintain a clear view of the water for onlookers. And a pedestrian passage links all open spaces from South Station to the North End. Ferries, water shuttles, cruise ships and yachts, fishing boats, whale watch ships, harbor tour boats, cargo ships and power boats populate the water while shops, restaurants and museums flourish on shore.

Since the 1950s, the North End and the Waterfront have been psychologically and, to a certain extent, physically cut off from the rest of Central Boston by an ugly, green, steel overpass, part of the Central Artery. The overpass has been a blight on the North End since its inception. But all that will change early in the new millenium when the Central Artery Project to put the highway under Boston is completed. The steel will come down, reuniting the North End with Central Boston.

Area Code: 617

Zip Codes: 02113, 02109

Post Offices: McCormack Station, Post Office Square, 90 Devonshire Street, 720-3050.

Police District: District A1, Area A, 40 New Sudbury Street, 343-4627 (Community Officer).

Emergency Hospital: Mass General Hospital, 32 Fruit Street, 726-2000.

Libraries: North End Branch, 25 Parmenter Street, 227-8135.

Public School Education: Eliot Elementary, 16 Charter Street, 635-8545.

Public Transportation: Blue Line at Aquarium; Orange and Green Lines at Haymarket; Red Line at South Station. Buses: 6 Boston Marine Industrial Park-Haymarket & South Station, 7 City Point-Downtown, 92 Assembly Square Mall-Downtown, 93 Sullivan-Downtown, 111 Woodlawn-Haymarket.

CHARLESTOWN

Boundaries: North: the Mystic River; **East:** Boston Harbor; **South:** Boston Harbor and the Charles River; **West:** Caldwell Street, Crescent Street and Inner Belt Industrial Park.

Charlestown is a great example of the success of urban renewal projects and the political power available to community groups committed to a neighborhood. It has the same colonial feel as Beacon Hill but it costs much less to live here. A national historic district, Charlestown also has masonry rowhouses, cobblestone streets, gas-lit street lights and is located on a hill which offers spectacular views. Residents call Charlestown "Boston's Oldest Village." Paul Revere's famous ride is recreated every April 17th with the Revere role played by a living relative.

Located across the Charles River from downtown Boston, Charlestown was settled in 1629 by John Winthrop and became part of Boston in 1874. Because the British burned the eastern section of the town to the ground in 1775, the oldest surviving buildings in Charlestown date back only to the 1780s. The Warren Tavern on Pleasant Street, built in 1780, is the oldest tavern in New England and is still open for business.

The Charlestown Navy Yard was originally established in the early 1800s. During World War II, waves of immigrants, sailors and itinerant laborers arrived in Charlestown to produce warships. Many family homes were converted into rooming houses and Charlestown's reputation suffered, especially during the post-war depression.

Charlestown turned itself around in the mid-1970s. Community groups fought successfully against development schemes to tear down historic buildings and put up skyscrapers in their place. The ugly, noisy, elevated train was dismantled. Urban renewal projects succeeded in beautifying the neighborhood so well that young professionals started moving in during the 1980s. The Charlestown Navy Yard, a community in itself, is still under conversion and has become a desirable and pricey address.

Charlestown still has a substantial and close-knit Irish-American population established in the 1800s when Irish immigrants came to work on the railroads. However, a newcomer population is also well represented. Many people relocate to the Monument area, downtown, and the Navy Yard if they can afford it. Newcomers may feel most comfortable moving into these areas.

Charlestown is divided into a number of smaller designations. The

Navy Yard is still a working port with restaurants, water shuttles to Long Wharf in Boston, and large, upscale housing complexes offering spectacular views of the Atlantic. Thompson Square is two triangles of landscaped park on the south side of Bunker Hill. City Square is close to Thompson Square and is where much of the eastern part of the community shops. Monument Square circles Bunker Hill Monument and is home to larger houses built in the 1850s. The Schraffts tower area is close to Sullivan Square, a traffic circle where much of Charlestown's public transportation converges. As part of the Central Artery project, the traffic circle at Charlestown Square has been converted into a traditional intersection feeding into I-93 and the Charlestown Bridge.

Charlestown is cozy and accessible. Residents can travel to Boston by foot, bike, bus, boat or train and can reach Somerville and Cambridge by bike, bus and train. Parking is tight around the Monument and downtown but elsewhere it is much easier and there are no resident sticker parking restrictions.

Charlestown remains an exciting place to live, with many residents involved in renovation projects — from individual condos and apartments being rehabilitated by small landlords to major fixups by the community's numerous community and landmark organizations.

Area Code: 617

Zip Code: 02129

Post Offices: 1 Thompson Square, 242-7125.

Police District: District A15, Area A, 40 New Sudbury Street, 343-4627 (Community Officer).

Emergency Hospital: Mass General Hospital, 32 Fruit Street, 726-2000.

Libraries: Charlestown Branch, 179 Main Street, 242-1248.

Public School Education: North Zone: Harvard/Kent Elementary, 50 Bunker Hill Street, 635-8358; Warren/Prescott Elementary, 50 School Street, 635-8346; Edwards Middle School, 28 Walker Street, 635-8516; Charlestown High, 240 Medford Street, 635-9914; Fenway Middle College High, 250 Rutherford Avenue, 635-9911.

Public Transportation: Orange Line at Community College and Sullivan Square. Buses: 111 Woodlawn-Haymarket, 92 Assembly Square Mall-Downtown, 93 Sullivan-Downtown, 86 Sullivan-

Cleveland Circle, 91 Sullivan-Central Square. Navy Yard Water Shuttle to Long Wharf.

BACK BAY

Boundaries: North: the Charles River; **East:** Arlington Street; **South:** the Mass Turnpike; **West:** Charlesgate East.

This neighborhood used to be a bay — actually a tidal flat — of the Charles River. It became Back Bay in an impressive landfill project that took nearly 25 years to complete, beginning at the Public Garden in 1857 and ultimately filling 400 acres by the 1880s.

Back Bay was developed by the affluent for the affluent, and it offers some of the City's most expensive housing. Young professionals, wealthy students, a highbrow crowd and some of Boston's oldest families live in Back Bay.

Back Bay is a planned community of Victorian architecture based on the French model with a central boulevard. The neighborhood is centered around Commonwealth Avenue, a 200-foot-wide central boulevard that runs from the Fens to the Public Garden. This means Back Bay inhabitants see a lot of green space. Many outstanding architects had a hand in designing this neighborhood. It is the largest example of Victorian architecture and city planning left in the nation.

Unfortunately, Back Bay went through a de-gentrification period after the city's post-WWII-depression and before the city's recognition of the importance of historical sites in the 1970s. Developers bought houses and converted them into apartments, schools, and dormitories. You will find expensive pits designed to trap the student population here. Many Back Bay apartments are oddly configured because developers from this era wanted to fit in as many apartments as possible. Then, during the condo-conversions in the early 1970s, many as yet untouched buildings were gutted and the elaborate French moldings were destroyed.

However, if you look hard you can find apartments with original fixtures. Back Bay clearly has spectacular, architecturally interesting housing if you can afford it. And if you prefer modern housing you can find high and low-rise apartments around the Prudential Center. As with most downtown Boston neighborhoods, this one is also a National Historic District. Copley Square is home to Trinity Church and South Church as well as Boston Public Library's main branch.

Parking is just as tight in Back Bay as it is on Beacon Hill and resident sticker restrictions apply. Residents in the eastern section of the neighborhood might find it convenient to park in the newly renovated Boston Common Parking Garage.

Back Bay is a convenient place to live, with many amenities including its proximity to the Public Garden, Boston Common, the Charles River, and the Fens. It also has some of the city's most interesting shopping. Newbury Street is filled with boutiques, cafes and galleries where you can find one-of-a-kind treasures. Boylston Street is home to some of the major shopping names (Lord & Taylor, etc.). The Prudential Center and Copley Place contain a hotel complex and both have indoor shopping malls. Back Bay also has a large supermarket, many delis, hardware stores, music stores, sporting goods stores and an impressive number of good restaurants.

One thing newcomers might find odd about Bostonians is their relationship to the city's skyscrapers. Back Bay has two, the Prudential Center and the John Hancock building, and residents complain about the aesthetic of having them for neighbors. The John Hancock building may actually shade your living room if you live too close to it. And neither building really fits in with the architectural scheme of the neighborhood. Nevertheless, they've both become proud Back Bay landmarks.

Area Code: 617

Zip Codes: 02115, 02116

Post Offices: Astor Station, 207 Mass. Ave., 247-3055. Back Bay Branch, 390 Stuart Street, 542-0160. Boston University Branch, 775 Commonwealth Avenue, 266-8979. Prudential Center Branch, 800 Boylston Street, 267-8162.

Police District: District D4, Area D, 7 Warren Avenue, 343-4457 (Community Officer).

Emergency Hospitals: Mass General Hospital, 32 Fruit Street, 724-4123. Boston City Hospital, 818 Harrison Avenue, 534-4929.

Libraries: Central Library, Copley Square, main entrance located at 666 Boylston Street, 536-5400.

Public Transportation: Green Line. Orange Line at Back Bay Station. Buses: 9 City Point-Copley Square, 10 City Point-Copley Square, 39 Forest Hills-Back Bay, 55 Queensberry-Copley Square/Park and Tremont Streets.

SOUTH END

Boundaries: North: Herald Street/the Mass Turnpike; **East:** Albany Street/Fitzgerald Expressway; **Southeast and Southwest:** Melnea Cass Boulevard; **West:** Huntington Avenue.

Like those in the Back Bay, the South End's tidal flats were filled in during the mid-1800s. This neighborhood's Victorian architecture was built in the English style. In contrast to Back Bay's central boulevard, the South End was designed around squares, oblong parks surrounded by brownstone rowhouses. The South End is also a National Historic District.

This neighborhood has been one of the city's most socially and racially diverse areas since the turn of the century and continues to be so today. Irish, Jewish, Italian, Chinese, Greek, Syrian and Lebanese immigrants have all made the South End their home at one time or another. It is also home to a large African-American and Latino/Hispanic population.

Unfortunately the same apartment conversion process that occurred in Back Bay also happened here. Many of the Victorian brownstones have been chopped up into small apartments. However, there are some decent sized apartments left and it's not rare to find digs with a working fireplace and original fixtures. Check out the St. Botolph's area to get an idea of what things were once like.

The South End also has its share of creative shopping. The funk factor is higher here than in Back Bay and you will find eclectic shops, antique dealers and galleries. You will also find some of the finest hybrid-ethnic and non-ethnic food in the city in the Clarendon, Columbus and West Newton Street areas. South End has all the conveniences of city living — dry cleaners, hardware stores, drug stores, corner markets. Copley Square is just as accessible to South End as it is to Back Bay and the Symphony area is nearby. Additionally, this neighborhood is home to the Cyclorama and the Boston Center for the Arts.

The South End is a bit more affordable than Back Bay but it is still relatively expensive. And although it has become fashionable, the neighborhood is still fighting a tough image. As a newcomer you may feel safest if you stay in the section between Tremont Street and Huntington Avenue. Once you've lived in South End for a while you'll determine your comfort zone and make your own decisions about safety.

Many types of people call the South End home. As mentioned, it is diverse ethnically. You'll find multigenerational blue collar families, artists, musicians and music students, a sizable gay population, young families and young professionals.

In addition to the neighborhood's many squares, its residents enjoy using Southwest Corridor Park. Public garden plots are also available in South End.

Area Code: 617

Zip Code: 02118

Post Offices: Prudential Center Branch, 800 Boylston Street, 267-8162. South End Branch, 59 West Dedham Street, 266-8613.

Police District: District D4, Area D, 7 Warren Avenue, 343-4457 (Community Officer).

Emergency Hospital: Boston City Hospital, 818 Harrison Avenue, 534-4929.

Libraries: South End Branch, 685 Tremont Street, 536-8241. Central Library, Copley Square, main entrance at 666 Boylston Street, 536-5400.

Public School Education: North Zone: Blackstone Elementary, 380 Shawmut Avenue, 635-8471; Hurley Elementary, 70 Worcester Street, 635-8489; Dearborn Middle School, 35 Greenville Street, 635-8412; Boston High, 152 Arlington Street, 635-8937.

Public Transportation: Orange Line. Buses: 1 Harvard-Dudley Square, 8 UMass-Ruggles Station, 8A Dudley Square-Kenmore Station, 9 City Point-Copley Square, 10 City Point-Copley Square, 39 Forest Hills-Back Bay, 43 Ruggles Station-Park & Tremont Streets, 47 Central Square-Albany Street, 49 Dudley Square-Downtown.

ALLSTON–BRIGHTON

Boundaries: North: Charles River; **East:** City of Brookline; **West:** City of Newton.

Allston/Brighton is a large section of Boston whose close proximity to Boston University, Boston College and convenient bus transportation to Harvard makes it attractive to many students. However, there are many non-student sections and the area offers some of Boston's most affordable housing.

The boundaries between Allston and Brighton are fuzzy. Some consider Allston the area north of Beacon Street and Brighton Avenue. Some delegate Allston only to the area north of the turnpike. In any case, the section connecting Allston/Brighton to the rest of Boston along the Charles River (the Boston University area) is usually considered Allston.

Established in 1635 with colonial land grants, the Allston/Brighton area was mostly agricultural until the late 1800s when the area established its stockyards as the major cattle market in New England. Allston was home to stockyards, slaughterhouses and meatpacking, an industry made possible by the Charles River and the railroad. Eventually the stockyards declined and other industries replaced them.

Once Back Bay was filled in the street cars were extended to Allston/Brighton. Good quality residential structures were built and many of them still exist today. The Brighton Center area has Victorian homes and a Catholic institutional belt (Boston College, etc.); Commonwealth Avenue was built up into a high density apartment district along the trolley line; the Cleveland Circle area features Art Deco apartments; and the rest of Brighton has mostly two-family homes and triple deckers.

Today, Allston/Brighton is an industrial/suburban community with affordable housing. This neighborhood houses a mixture of blue collar and other ethnic groups as well as a large student population. The mixture works well together: you can take advantage of the benefits of having the student population in the neighborhood (i.e. nightlife) without having to live in student areas. Allston/Brighton is young. A recent census reported that 69% of the region's population is between 15 and 34 years old.

Allston/Brighton has everything you need for services and goods. You'll find a large number of hardware, sporting goods, antique, carpet and furniture stores, a wide variety of restaurants, pubs and taverns, and several southeast Asian food stores and restaurants. Shopping areas are along Commonwealth Avenue, Brighton Avenue/Beacon Street, Harvard Street, Cambridge Street, and Washington Street. You'll find Boston's cheapest eats in Allston/Brighton.

Even though the neighborhood exhibits the influence of its Irish-Catholic heritage, the area is mixed racially and ethnically. Irish, Italian, Greek, Jewish, Asian, African-American and Hispanic populations can all be found in this part of Boston. Brighton shares a Jewish community with Brookline. Harvard Street, which runs through both Brookline and Brighton, is the main artery of Boston area Jewish culture.

Allston is more industrial and still battles a slightly seedy image. Many people who go to Allston for shopping and nightlife wouldn't feel comfortable living there and newcomers are advised to investigate Allston areas carefully before signing a lease. Commonwealth Avenue, featuring the Green Line, houses a large student population and might also be an area for the newcomer to avoid, although it is convenient to wait for the Green Line right at your front window in the winter months.

Brighton has various residential communities and subdivides itself in a number of ways. Newcomers would most likely feel comfortable in the following neighborhoods. **Brighton Center** is the area where Market Street intersects with Washington. **Oak Square** is where Faneuil Street intersects with Washington. The **North Beacon/Market** area is a blue collar neighborhood with condo complexes. **Cleveland Circle,** in the heart of Boston College territory, is beautiful. This area borders Brookline and is located next to the Chestnut Hill Reservoir. Many people think Cleveland Circle is actually in Brookline.

Be advised, the winter parking wars in Brighton are as fierce as they are anywhere else in the city. Parking is with resident sticker only in the densely populated areas but is not required everywhere.

Area Code: 617

Zip Codes: 02134, 02135

Post Offices: Allston Branch, 47 Harvard Avenue, 789-4273. Boston University, 775 Commonwealth Avenue, 266-8979. Brighton Branch, 424 Washington Street, 254-3387.

Police District: District D14, Area D, Brighton Neighborhood Station, 301 Washington Street, 343-4260.

Emergency Hospital: St. Elizabeth's, 736 Cambridge Street, 789-3000.

Libraries: Brighton Branch, 40 Academy Hill Road, 782-6032. Faneuil Street Branch, 419 Faneuil Street, 782-6705.

Public School Education: North Zone: Baldwin Elementary, 121 Corey Road, 635-8460; Early Learning Center, 40 Armington Street, 635-8409; Gardner Elementary, 30 Athol Street, 635-8365; Garfield Elementary, 95 Beechcroft Street, 635-8351; Hamilton Elementary, 198 Strathmore Road, 635-8388; Jackson/Mann Elementary, 40 Armington Street, 635-8532; Lyon Elementary, 50 Beechcroft Street, 635-7945; Winship Elementary School, 54 Dighton Street,

635-8399; Edison Middle School, 60 Glenmont Road, 635-8436; Taft Middle School, 20 Warren Street, 635-8428; Brighton High, 25 Warren Street, 635-9873; Horace Mann School for the Deaf and Hard of Hearing, 40 Arlington Street, 635-8534.

Public Transportation: Green Line "B" and "C" Buses: 51 Cleveland Circle-Forest Hills, 57 Watertown Square-Kenmore, 64 Oak Square-Central Square, 65 Brighton Center-Kenmore, 66 Harvard Square-Dudley Square, 86 Sullivan-Cleveland Circle, 301 Brighton Center-Downtown Express.

JAMAICA PLAIN

Boundaries: North: Huntington Avenue and Tremont; **East:** Columbus Avenue area; **South:** Allandale Street, Arnold Arboretum and South Street; **West:** the City of Brookline (Riverway and Chestnut Street areas).

Over the years Jamaica Plain has been transformed into a thoroughly democratic place to live. Originally a summer-resort area for Boston's colonial and federal-era rich and famous, it now houses one of Boston's most liberal and diverse communities. "Scenic" Jamaica Plain, once called the "Eden of America," has four community centers, more neighborhood associations and crime watch groups than any other area in Boston, and more open green space than any section of Boston.

Jamaica Plain (called "JP" by most residents) was part of Roxbury until West Roxbury included it in its secession of 1851. By 1873, West Roxbury voted to annex itself to Boston and Jamaica Plain was included in the deal.

This neighborhood benefited greatly from Boston's park building boom in the late 1800s. A large portion of the park system, known as the **Emerald Necklace**, is both in Jamaica Plain proper or adjacent to it. Benjamin Bussey left 250 acres to Harvard in 1842 which later became the Arnold Arboretum. Jamaica Pond was saved from certain pollution by the ice house industry when the city bought it for the Emerald Necklace. The ice houses and family estates came down, and this glacial kettle hole is now the cleanest body of fresh water in Boston. Franklin Park and Zoo is just south and west of the neighborhood.

Today Jamaica Plain is where politics lean to the left, artists and seamstresses sell their wares in front of the Arts Center on Centre Street, garden spots are available, and the community festivals are multi-cultural. Jamaica Plain is more like the Harvard and Central Square areas of Cambridge than any other Boston neighborhood.

Home to the largest Hispanic community in Boston, this neighborhood also houses a thriving African-American population, a large number of artists, writers, musicians, and graduate students from Harvard Medical School, Northeastern University and Boston University, as well as gay and lesbian citizens, and young professionals of all races. Although Jamaica Plain is young overall, there are enough senior citizens present to make this neighborhood a true community.

Jamaica Plain has a number of public transportation options, a fact reflected in the number of neighborhood households that do not have access to motor vehicles: 46%. Housing is relatively affordable in Jamaica Plain, but, of course, prices are on the rise, and apartment options are mostly one to three family houses. There are some rowhouses along Centre Street, some public housing, and one expensive high rise (Jamaica Towers). But Jamaica Plain has many triple deckers and Victorian era houses and has existing examples of Greek Revival, Italianate, Mansard, Queen Anne and Colonial Revival architecture.

Jamaica Plain's commercial spine is located along Centre Street/South Street. It has an Arts Center located in the old firehouse, an array of neighborhood pubs, interesting food, more than enough cafes, eclectic boutiques, and all the helpful services you might need. Although the neighborhood has food markets, natural food stores, and a large Hispanic supermarket (Hi Lo in Hyde Square where you can get an amazing variety of peppers), there are no conventional supermarkets.

Like the South End, JP still struggles with a tough reputation. Newcomers will feel more comfortable in the west, along the Brookline edge, until they've acclimated and determined a comfort level. The Jackson Square area has seen its share of violence and newcomers might not feel comfortable there. Try the pondside area, the western section of central Jamaica Plain, the area between the Arboretum and South Street, and Sumner Hill. Forest Hills also has some pleasant housing options.

Winter parking can be difficult on the more densely populated streets. Resident sticker parking is the exception but some sections do require it.

Area Code: 617

Zip Code: 02130

Post Offices: Jamaica Plain Branch, 655 Centre Street, 524-0402.

Police District: District E18, Area E Police Headquarters, 1708

Centre Street, West Roxbury, Community Officer 343-4564. Hyde Park-Jamaica Plain, 1249 Hyde Park Avenue, Hyde Park, 343-5600.

Emergency Hospitals: Beth Israel Hospital, 330 Brookline Avenue, 735-5397. Brigham and Women's Hospital, 680 Francis Avenue, 732-5640. Children's Hospital, 300 Longwood Avenue, 735-6624. Faulkner Hospital, 1153 Centre Street, 522-5800.

Libraries: Connolly Branch, 433 Centre Street, 522-1960. Jamaica Plain Branch, 12 Sedgwick (corner of South), 524-2053.

Public School Education: West Zone: Agassiz Elementary, 20 Child Street, 635-8198; Curley Elementary, 40 Pershing Road, 635-8239; Early Learning Center/West, 200 Heath Street, 635-8275; Fuller Elementary, 25 Glen Road, 635-8221; Hennigan Elementary, 200 Heath Street, 635-8264; Kennedy Elementary, 7 Bolster Street, 635-8127; Manning Elementary, Louder's Lane, 635-8102; Curley Middle School, 493 Centre Street, 635-8176; English High, 144 McBride Street, 635-8979; Greater Egleston Community High, 3134 Washington Street, 524-2555.

Public Transportation: Green Line only as far as Heath Street. Orange Line. Buses: 38 Wren Street-Forest Hills Station, 39 Forest Hills-Back Bay, 41 Centre & Eliot Streets-Dudley, 48 Centre & Eliot Streets-J.P. Loop.

ROSLINDALE

Boundaries: North: VFW Parkway and Arnold Arboretum; **East:** Forest Hills Cemetery and Mt. Hope Cemetery; **South:** Stony Brook Reservation, Poplar Street, Mansur Street, Cliffmont Street; **West:** West Roxbury Parkway and Centre Street.

Roslindale was also a part of the 1873 West Roxbury annexation to Boston. This area was very rural until the streetcars were extended to Roslindale Square in the late 1880s. Consisting mostly of hilly upland, Roslindale is a classic streetcar suburb with fine examples of turn of the century institutional architectural styles.

Roslindale experienced two building booms; the first in the 1890s and the second in the 1920s and 1930s. Public churches, schools and institutional buildings built during these time periods are all still extant and have been the focus of the Roslindale Village Main Street program, a project sponsored by the National Trust for Historic Preservation.

This neighborhood is a beautiful, moderate density residential area: over 75% of its housing stock consists of 1-4 unit buildings, usually with backyards. It's close to the Arboretum and Stony Brook Reservation with the Mt. Hope Cemetery also offering a green break. Although many buses feed commuters to the Forest Hills train station and the commuter rail stops at Roslindale Center, most residents find it difficult to live in Roslindale without a car.

Roslindale Center is the heart of the community and Washington Street serves as its commercial spine. With outstanding Greek bakeries, some decent restaurants and diners, an indoor community pool, accessible green space, and all the necessary daily services (hardware stores, video stores, etc.), Roslindale lacks only nightlife. But such excitement is readily available elsewhere and many residents just go to Jamaica Plain. After all, you don't move to Roslindale for nightlife, you move here for the big backyards and the easy parking. Roslindale does not suffer the winter parking wars that most of Boston endures during the cold months, mostly because there are a large number of driveways.

Roslindale rents are cheaper than Jamaica Plain; you really do get more bang for the buck. But, as mentioned, commuting around town with mass transit isn't as easy and the commuter rail disrupts Roslindale's traffic flow because of the large number of dead-end and one-way streets. You have to know where the underpasses are which can make getting around a challenge. It's also a true test of how well you know your neighborhood!

This area is predominantly white but Hispanic and African-American populations are on the rise. Roslindale's ethnic groups do mix and are quite comfortable with each other. The community has 25 active crime watches, garden spots for rent and four playground areas: Adams Park, Healy Playground, Parkman Playground, and Fallon Field.

Roslindale is broken up into the following divisions: Centre-South, Village-Lower Washington, Mount Hope, and Metropolitan Hill-Beech.

Area Code: 617

Zip Code: 02131

Post Offices: Roslindale Branch, 16 Cummins Highway, 323-3975.

Police District: District E5, Area E, West Roxbury/Roslindale, 1708 Centre Street, West Roxbury, 343-4564 (Community Officer).

Emergency Hospital: Faulkner Hospital, 1153 Centre Street, 522-5800.

Libraries: Roslindale Branch, 4238 Washington Street, 323-2343.

Public School Education: West Zone: Bates Elementary, 426 Beech Street, 635-8064; Conley Elementary School, 450 Poplar Street, 635-8099; Haley Elementary, 570 American Legion Highway, 635-8169; Mozart Elementary, 236 Beech Street, 635-8082; Philbrick Elementary, 40 Philbrick Street, 635-8069; Sumner Elementary, 15 Basile Street, 635-8131; Irving Middle School, 105 Cummins Highway, 635-8072.

Public Transportation: Orange Line at Forest Hills Station. Commuter Train at Roslindale Village. Buses: 14 Roslindale Square-Dudley Square, 30 Mattapan-Roslindale Square, 32 Wolcott Square-Forest Hills, 34 Dedham Line-Forest Hills, 34E Walpole Center-Forest Hills, 35 Dedham Mall/Stimson-Forest Hills, 36 Charles River-Forest Hills, 37 Baker & Vermont-Forest Hills, 50 Cleary Square-Forest Hills.

WEST ROXBURY

Boundaries: North: Allandale Street. **East:** West Roxbury Parkway and Centre Street. **South:** Suffolk County Line. **West:** City of Newton and City of Brookline

West Roxbury and Roslindale were once part of Roxbury, or "Rocksbury," established in 1630. Initially the area was sparsely settled by farming families. Later wealthy Boston families built their summer estates here. West Roxbury seceded from Roxbury, bringing Jamaica Plain and Roslindale along, in 1851. The area was annexed to Boston in 1874.

The oldest private grammar school in the country, the Roxbury Latin School established in 1645, is located here. Another historical monument in West Roxbury is Brook Farm, the utopian experimental community attempted by Bronson Alcott (Louisa May's father) and his band of merry transcendentalists. Brook Farm is now a Metropolitan District Commission park (MDC). West Roxbury actually has a Paleozoic volcano at the intersection of Washington and Grove Streets.

West Roxbury underwent several subdivisions during the post-Civil War era which led to real estate developers gaining a powerful voice in local politics. Their influence led to West Roxbury annexing itself to Boston. Streetcar lines and railroad tracks were extended to the area in the 1890s and residential development grew rapidly. Multi-family housing was introduced during this era.

Today West Roxbury is Boston's most suburban neighborhood with a predominantly white (95%) population, a median age of 35 years (median age in Boston is 28.8), and a profusion of single family homes with huge backyards. It also has some pretty incredible apartments. The neighborhood has political muscle, efficient services and crime-free streets. More like Brookline than Boston, West Roxbury is more expensive to live in than Jamaica Plain and Roslindale but cheaper than Newton and Brookline. It's hard to live here without a car, but fortunately parking is never a problem.

West Roxbury is divided up as follows: Bellevue-Hill, Spring-Upper Washington, Highlands, and Brook Farm-Parkway. In addition to Brook Farm, the neighborhood has MDC park facilities along the VFW and West Roxbury Parkways. Its recreational facilities, Hynes and Billings, were rehabbed recently and the City plans to improve access to the Charles River shoreline.

Residents enjoy many interesting stores and restaurants and have access to shopping all along Route 1. Most will drive to Dedham rather than Boston for anything they can't find in West Roxbury.

Area Code: 617

Zip Code: 02132

Post Offices: West Roxbury Branch, 1970 Centre Street, 325-0058.

Police District: District E5, Area E, 1708 Centre Street, 343-4564 (Community Officer).

Emergency Hospital: Faulkner Hospital, 1153 Centre Street, 522-5800.

Libraries: West Roxbury Branch, 1961 Centre Street, 325-3147.

Public School Education: West Zone: Beethoven Elementary, 5125 Washington Street, 635-8149; Kilmer Elementary, 35 Baker Street, 635-8060; Lyndon Elementary, 140 Russett Road, 635-6824; Ohrenberger Elementary, 175 West Boundary Road, 635-8157; Shaw Middle School, 20 Mt. Vernon Street, 635-8050; West Roxbury High, 1205 VFW Parkway, 635-8917.

Public Transportation: Buses: 36 Charles River-Forest Hills, 37 Baker & Vermont-Forest Hills, 38 Wren Street-Forest Hills, 52 Dedham Mall/Charles River-Watertown Square.

EAST BOSTON

Boundaries: North: Suffolk Downs. **East:** Bennington Street, Bayswater Street, Logan Airport. **West:** Marginal Street. **South:** Constitution Beach and Logan Airport.

East Boston, "Eastie" to residents, retains a strong link to its Italian-American roots, though several ethnic groups are beginning to make inroads in that dominance. Since the 1980s, the Hispanic community especially has grown here.

East Boston offers a wide variety of shops and restaurants that line the narrow streets, evident in the ethnic businesses in Maverick Square. Just off Route 1A out of the Callahan-Sumner Tunnel is Santarpio's, a landmark restaurant that provides a great old neighborhood feel.

Eastie has been part of Boston since 1637, but no part of it actually touches Boston proper. East Boston took shape after developers began filling in marshes between five islands.

One third of East Boston's area is taken up by Logan International Airport, one of the country's busiest. While noise pollution is a concern to residents living near Logan, the Massachusetts Port Authority has overseen a project to reduce the effects in area homes in East Boston, Winthrop, Revere and South Boston. Call the Massachusetts Port Authority for details at 561-1636.

For those who like to play the ponies, Suffolk Downs offers live horse racing and also closed circuit television broadcasts of cards from other tracks around the country.

There is also a large wetlands here, the Belle Isle Marsh, which gives an idea of what the area looked like during the 17th century.

A massive redevelopment of the East Boston waterfront has been proposed which would resemble what has taken place in Charlestown, across Boston Harbor. Plans call for housing, shopping areas and restaurants.

The densely-populated Eagle Hill section features old Victorian houses, accessible from Meridian Street. Along Sumner Street is Jeffries Point, with its two and three-family homes close to Boston Harbor. Brownstones can be found on Webster Street. The Orient Heights section offers a bit more room, with more single-family homes. Waterfront Park on Marginal Street offers a vivid view of Boston. It's close to Maverick Square, where MBTA buses and the Blue Line subway give one a quick way into the downtown area.

Another travel alternative to and from Boston is the commuter ferry which runs between the Lewis Street Wharf in East Boston and Long Wharf.

Area Code: 617

Zip Code: 02128

Post Offices: East Boston, 50 Meridian Street, 561-0760.

Police: East Boston, 69 Paris Street, 343-4220.

Emergency Hospitals: East Boston Neighborhood Health Center, 10 Gold Street, 569-5800.

Libraries: East Boston Branch, 276 Meridian Street, 569-0271, Orient Heights Branch, 18 Barnes Avenue, 567-2516.

Public School Education: North Zone: Adams Elementary, 165 Webster Street, 635-8383; Bradley Elementary, 10 Beachview Road, 635-8422; Guild Elementary School, 195 Leyden Street, 635-8523; Kennedy Elementary, 343 Saratoga Street, 635-8466; McKay Elementary & Middle School, 122 Cottage Street, 635-8510; O'Donnell Elementary, 33 Trenton Street, 635-8454; Otis Elementary, 218 Marion Street, 635-8372; Umana/Barnes Middle School, 312 Border Street, 635-8481; East Boston High, 86 White Street, 635-9896.

Public Transportation: The Blue Line. Buses: 112 East Boston-Chelsea-Everett-Medford, 116 East Boston-Chelsea-Revere, 117 East Boston-Chelsea-Revere, 120 Orient Heights-Maverick Station, 121 Wood Island-Maverick Station.

DORCHESTER

Boundaries: North: Columbia Road. **South:** Cummings Highway. **West:** Harvard Street, Franklin Park. **East:** Boston Harbor.

Dorchester is the largest section of Boston, with strong ties not only to Boston's rich past, but also to some of the key events in U.S. history. Some of the city's most beautiful Victorian homes were built in Dorchester, but the area is better known for its "triple-decker" three-family houses that were popular in the early 1900s in neighborhoods like Savin Hill.

Dorchester has a racially diverse population, ranging from Irish to Southeast Asian, Cape Verdian, African-American, Hispanic and Polish.

Dorchester Avenue, also known as "Dot Ave," is the main drag through the area, serving as home to Irish pubs and bakeries sitting beside Southeast Asian markets and West Indian grocers where some of the most fragrant curries and spices can be bought.

There are plenty of parks and other open space, including Franklin Park and the Franklin Park Zoo, which boasts a spectacular ape house.

Dorchester's history goes back to the Puritans landing at what is now known as Columbia Point, where the Kennedy Library and UMass Boston are located. The Puritans set up a fort on top of Savin Hill to guard against Indian raids. Patriots had a clear view of what the Redcoats were up to from Dorchester Heights during the Siege of Boston in 1776. This is where George Washington and his troops set up cannons and eventually helped persuade the British to flee for good. It is now a National Historic Site in Thomas Park, off Telegraph Street.

The city's oldest standing house, the 1648 Blake House on Columbia Road, is located near Edward Everett Square and the Dorchester North Burying Ground, which dates back to 1633. On Parish Street, on top of Meeting House Hill, is the Mather School, the nation's oldest elementary school, which was founded in 1639. Dorchester was annexed as a suburb of Boston in 1869, helped greatly by the development of the electric tram in 1857.

Other points of interest in Dorchester include the world's largest copyrighted work of art, a 150-foot high multi-colored painting on the Dorchester gas tank, which was designed by Corita Kent, a former nun in the Order of the Immaculate Conception.

Area Code: 617

Zip Codes: 02119; 02121, 02122, 02124; 02125

Post Offices: Dorchester Center, 450 Talbot Avenue, 825-7885; Dorchester Station, 210 Adams Street, 288-1219; Grove Hall, 647 Warren Street, 445-7594; Roxbury Station, 55 Roxbury Street, 427-7199; Uphams Corner Post Office, 551 Columbia Road, 287-0297.

Police District: Area C District 11, 40 Gibson Street, 343-4330.

Emergency Hospital: Carney Hospital, 2100 Dorchester Avenue, 296-4000.

Libraries: Adams Street Branch, 690 Adams Street, 436-6900; Codman Square Branch, 690 Washington Street, 436-6900; Fields Corner, 1520 Dorchester Avenue, 436-2155; Lower Mills, 27

Richmond Street, 298-7841; Uphams Corner, 500 Columbia Road, 265-0139.

Public School Education: East Zone: Clap Elementary, 35 Harvest Street, 635-8672; Dever Elementary, 325 Mt. Vernon, 635-8694; Early Learning Center/East, 370 Columbia Road, 635-8604; Endicott Elementary, 2 McLellan Street, 635-8648; Everett Elementary, 71 Pleasant Street, 635-8779; Fifield Elementary, 25 Dunbar Avenue, 635-8618; Sarah Greenwood Elementary and Middle School, 189 Glenway Street, 635-8710; Holland Elementary, 85 Olney Street, 635-8832; Holmes Elementary; 40 School Street, 635-8681; Kenny Elementary, 19 Oakton Avenue, 635-8789; Lee Elementary, 155 Talbot Avenue, 635-8687; Marshall Elementary, 35 Westville Street, 635-8810; Mather Elementary, One Parish Street, 635-8757; Murphy Elementary; One Worrell Street, 635-8781; O'Hearn Elementary, 1669 Dorchester Avenue, 635-8725; Russell Elementary, 750 Columbia Road, 635-8803; Shaw Elementary, 429 Norfolk Street, 635-8719; Stone Elementary, 22 Regina Road, 635-8773; Cleveland Middle School, 11 Charles Street, 635-8631; The Harbor School, Denney Youth Center, 576-1260; McCormack Middle School, 315 Mt. Vernon Street, 635-8657; Thompson Middle School, 100 Maxwell Street, 635-8764; Jeremiah Burke High, 60 Washington Street, 635-9837; Dorchester High, 9 Peacevale Road, 635-8904.

Public Transportation: Red Line. Buses: 210 Boston-Dorchester-Quincy, 215 Quincy-Milton-Dorchester-Boston, 217 Quincy-Milton-Dorchester-Boston, 238 Quincy-Braintree-Randolph-Dorchester-Boston, 240 Quincy, Braintree, Randolph-Avon-Dorchester-Boston, 245 Quincy-Milton-Dorchester-Boston.

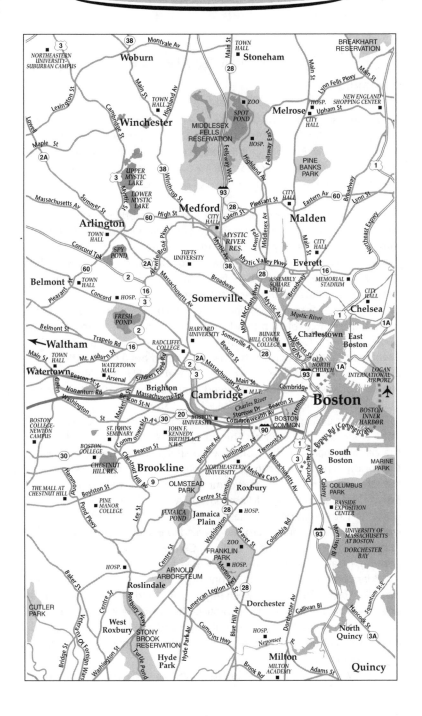

SURROUNDING COMMUNITIES

CAMBRIDGE

Boundaries: North and Northeast from west to east: Town of Arlington, Routes 2 and 16; City of Somerville, just east of Mass. Ave. then just west of Beacon until it intersects with Cambridge Street; just north of Cambridge Street. **South to Southwest:** the Charles River. **West:** Town of Watertown and Town of Belmont.

Cambridge, the one-time capital of the Massachusetts Bay Colony, is a large city consisting of approximately 100,000 people in a six square mile area with diverse neighborhoods. The city was founded as New Towne in 1630, changing its name to Cambridge in 1636. The Cambridge/Somerville boundary from Inman Square to East Cambridge is the oldest political boundary in the Boston area.

Cambridge features prominently in Revolutionary War history. One of its most noticeable landmarks is the place on Mason and Garden Streets where General Washington assumed command of the Revolutionary Army. Washington headquartered briefly on Brattle Street at a house now known as the Longfellow National Historic Site because Henry Wadsworth Longfellow lived there in the 1840s. It is now a Quaker meeting house and a popular tourist stop.

Harvard College, the oldest in the United States, was established in 1636 along the Charles River. The college quickly became the center of the city and maintained this status even after **Cambridgeport** and **East Cambridge** emerged as commercial centers during the 18th century. In the late 19th century civic and commercial business shifted to **Central Square,** located just down Massachusetts Avenue from Harvard Square. Boston's 19th century industrial development encouraged industry in Cambridge and various enterprises succeeded in North Cambridge, such as brickmaking and ice, and in East and Central Cambridge glass, candy, printing, meat packing and furniture were tried.

Massachusetts Institute of Technology (MIT) moved across the river from Boston in 1916, greatly changing the Kendall Square area and enlarging Cambridge's academic profile. The university is housed on 142 acres also along the Charles River but south and east of Harvard. Harvard and MIT created the environment that has made Cambridge a center of high technology.

Today Cambridge is home to professors, scientists, students, industrial workers, immigrants from around the world, techies and other professionals. And yes, ivy actually grows on the red brick buildings in Harvard Square. Cambridge blends academia with a thriving night life. Rents are relatively high but some areas are more reasonable than others.

This city enjoys an international flavor from two directions: it is home to thousands of foreign students and professors who live here during the school year as well as thousands of immigrants, many of whom are small business and restaurant owners.

Cambridge is closely tied to Somerville. Residents pass back and forth across the border, from square to square, quite frequently.

It's very easy to live in Cambridge without a car. There are many buses and the Red Line runs right down the length of the city. If you do have a car you'll struggle with parking, but you'll be happy with how accessible the area's major throughways are: Mass. Ave., Route 2 to Route 128, Route 16 and I-93 are all within reach.

Cambridge itself is also divided into smaller neighborhoods and squares. Following are brief profiles of Cambridge's many neighborhoods and squares traveling roughly east to west. They're linked by the Massachusetts Bay Transportation Authority's (MBTA) Red Line (subway), which has four stops in Cambridge, and by Mass. Ave., a commercial corridor loaded with shopping, that runs the length of Cambridge, continuing through Somerville and Arlington.

EAST CAMBRIDGE

Locals define East Cambridge as the area from the waterfront to the Cambridge Street railroad tracks. It has a diverse ethnic mix, many blue collar workers (although the number of manufacturing jobs has declined), and some of the most affordable rents in Cambridge (not counting the new, upscale condos on the waterfront). It's just a hop from here to downtown Boston.

Inman Square is located on East Cambridge's western boundary and Kendall Square is located on its southern boundary. The Cambridgeside Galleria Mall and new development on Cambridge Street have also brought the consumer to East Cambridge. Green space is available at Centanni Way Park and the Lechmere Canal Park. The **Wellington-Harrington** area is a densely populated section right near **Inman Square**. This region houses a large Hispanic, Portuguese and African-American population.

MIT AND KENDALL SQUARE

Just south of East Cambridge, sprawled along the Charles River, is the MIT neighborhood. Even though there's not a lot of residential housing in this area it deserves a quick overview. The first T stop in Cambridge, MIT covers 142 acres along the Charles. Kendall Square is located where Broadway and Main branch off just west of the Longfellow Bridge. Home to the MIT Press Book Sale Annex, this square seems to shut down at dusk when the 9-to-5-ers who use it head home after work. However, just a few blocks away, 1 Kendall Square offers a lively dining and entertainment scene well into the night. This area is home to much high-tech industry.

INMAN SQUARE

Inman Square, located at the junction of Cambridge and Hampshire Streets, is the only Cambridge square without a T stop. It borders Somerville and covers small sections of East Cambridge, Mid-Cambridge and Area 4. It's only a few blocks south of Somerville's Union Square.

Inman Square's reputation with outsiders is built on its numerous international restaurants. However, this is really the one square in Cambridge that remains a neighborhood hangout rather than a magnet for the trendy. It has coffee shops, a bakery, a women's bookstore, and a quiet night scene.

AREA 4

Located in the heart of Cambridge's east side, Area 4 has the reputation of being Cambridge's toughest neighborhood. However, the community is fighting back. A new Area 4 Youth Center opened recently and has succeeded in getting some kids off the streets.

Central Square is on Area 4's western edge. This neighborhood has the largest African-American and Hispanic population in Cambridge and is home to *El Mundo*, Massachusetts' oldest Spanish newspaper. The area has many ethnic specialty and food markets, international restaurants, and Sennet Park, where free concerts and street fairs are often held.

CENTRAL SQUARE

The Red Line's next stop after Kendall Square is in Central Square where Area 4, Cambridgeport and Mid-Cambridge all meet. Western Avenue, River Street and Magazine Street converge at Massachusetts Avenue and at this tangle of commerce and traffic lies Central Square, home to Cambridge's municipal business.

You'll find City Hall, the police station and the main post office branch here. You'll also find the YMCA, the YWCA, a homeless shelter, the Dance Complex building, Dance Umbrella and a number of nightclubs offering a diverse menu of music, poetry and food.

This mixture of night life and social services give Central Square its unique flavor. Central Square is funky. It has been described as both "dirty and dangerous" and as a welcome refuge from the bland commercialization of Harvard Square.

CAMBRIDGEPORT AND RIVERSIDE

These neighborhoods are located along the Charles River and are a sort of transitional area between the Harvard-influenced western part of Cambridge and the eastern industrial section. Central Square is on Riverside's eastern edge and Cambridgeport's northern.

Riverside's western edge houses many of Harvard's dorms but the neighborhood loses its ivy influence as you head east. The presence of these dorms makes the overall median age for the neighborhood young. However, there is a sizable African-American and Asian population here which gives the area a sense of community despite its seasonal inhabitants.

Cambridgeport, a popular place for immigrants and non-immigrants alike, has lost much land to MIT. It has many triple deckers and pocket parks as well as an MDC recreational facility along Magazine Beach. Both neighborhoods are in transition and are slowly being gentrified.

MID-CAMBRIDGE AND AGASSIZ

North of Riverside, but west of Area 4, Mid-Cambridge has Harvard Square on the west and Inman Square on the east. Mid-Cambridge has the most residents of any Cambridge community and houses the Main Branch of the Cambridge Public Library.

North of Mid-Cambridge and with Somerville on its eastern edge, Agassiz has the brick lined streets you think of when you think of Cambridge. It also has a highly educated population: over 80 percent of Agassiz residents have college or graduate degrees. **Porter Square** is located on its northern border.

Both neighborhoods are quiet, residential communities.

HARVARD SQUARE

Harvard Square, the third Cambridge T stop and the second Cambridge Square located on Mass. Ave., is located in Mid-Cambridge but it spills into West Cambridge, Riverside and Neighborhood 9.

Known for bookstores, street musicians and college culture, Harvard Square is home to an amazing array of sights, sounds, shops, newspapers, events, restaurants and history. The city licenses over 300 street performers which makes any summer evening on the Square a cheap night of entertainment. Many famous performers (including Bob Dylan and Tracy Chapman) began their careers performing here.

People-watching is a favorite Harvard Square activity. Coffee is abundant. Music stores proliferate. So do poetry readings, lectures, and earnest political discussions. You'll find jazz, folk and rock music at the area nightclubs and bars, movie houses, repertory theater, smoke-free alcohol-free dances and a wide array of museums.

WEST CAMBRIDGE AND NEIGHBORHOOD 9

Located south of Neighborhood 9 and west of Harvard Square, West Cambridge has the most green space of any neighborhood in Cambridge. It's bordered by the Charles, the Mt. Auburn Cemetery, Fresh Pond and the Cambridge Common. People who are able to move into West Cambridge stick around for a while. The *Cambridge Chronicle* reports that over 50 percent of this neighborhood's residents have lived in the same residence since 1985. This neighborhood is home to many Revolutionary War historic sites, including the Longfellow House. Brattle Street possesses an amazing array of gorgeous mansions.

Neighborhood 9 is located in the heart of western Cambridge. West Cambridge and Neighborhood 9 are the most affluent neighborhoods in Cambridge.

NORTH CAMBRIDGE

North Cambridge's commercial business is found along Mass. Ave. and in Porter Square. This area also has much green space: the Clarendon Avenue Playground, Linear Park, Rindge Field, Gergin Playground and the O'Callaghan Little League field.

PORTER SQUARE

Porter Square is the third Cambridge square on Mass. Ave. and the fourth Cambridge T stop on the Red Line. It is closely tied to Davis Square in Somerville, the very next Red Line T stop.

Porter Square is home to Porter Square Shopping Mall, the Porter Exchange Mall (housed in the old Sears Building) and the Porter Arcade which inhabits an old auto dealership. The Exchange Mall has a marvelous Asian food court with sushi and noodle bars and everything in-between.

The Square offers a suburban-style parking lot and a T station. Mass. Ave. features numerous little shops selling all sorts of unique items as well as some major name stores. The Square also contains several popular restaurants and health clubs.

Area Code: 617

Zip Codes: Agassiz, West Cambridge and Neighborhood 9 - 02138, North Cambridge - 02140, Cambridgeport - 02139, East Cambridge - 02141 and 02142

Post Offices: Cambridge Central, 770 Mass. Ave., 876-0602. East Cambridge, 3030 Cambridge Street, 876-6484. Harvard Square, 125 Mt. Auburn Street, 876-6483. Inman Square, 1309 Cambridge Street, 864-4262. Kendall Square, 250 Main Street, 876-6180. MIT 84 Mass. Ave., 494-8999. North Cambridge, 1953 Mass. Ave., 876-8162. Soldiers Field Branch, 16 N. Harvard Street, 354-6535.

Police: Cambridge Police, 5 Western Avenue, 349-3390 (Community Services)

Emergency Hospitals: Cambridge Hospital, 1493 Cambridge Street, 498-1000. Mt. Auburn Hospital, 330 Mt. Auburn Street, 492-3500.

Libraries: Main, 499 Broadway, 349-4040. Boudreau/Observatory

Hill, 245 Concord Avenue, 349-4017. Central Square, 45 Pearl Street, 349-4010. Collins/Mt. Auburn, 64 Aberdeen Avenue, 349-4021. North Cambridge, 70 Rindge Avenue, 349-4023. O'Connell/East Cambridge, 48 Sixth Street, 349-4019. Valente/Cambridge Field, 826 Cambridge Street, 349-4015.

Public School Education: Agassiz Elementary, 28 Sacramento Street, 349-6525; Fitzgerald, 70 Rindge Avenue, 349-6530; Fletcher Elementary, 89 Elm Street, 349-6865; Graham & Parks School, 15 Upton Street, 349-6612; Haggerty, 110 Cushing, 349-6555; Harrington Elementary, 850 Cambridge Street, 349-6540; Maynard Elementary, 225 Windsor Street, 349-6588; Kennedy School, 158 Spring Street, 349-6841; King School, 100 Putnam Avenue, 349-6562; Longfellow, 359 Broadway, 349-6875; Morse Elementary, 40 Granite Street, 349-6575; Peabody School, 44 Linnaean Street, 349-6577; Togin School, 197 Vassal Lane, 349-6600; The Cambridge Rindge & Latin School, 459 Broadway, 349-6630.

Public Transportation: The Red Line. Buses: 1 Harvard-Dudley Square, 47 Central Square-Albany Street, 64 Oak Square-Central Square, 66 Harvard Square-Dudley Square, 69 Harvard-Lechmere, 70 Cedarwood-Central Square, 70A North Waltham-Central Square, 74 Belmont Center-Harvard, 77 Arlington Heights-Harvard Station, 77A North Cambridge-Harvard Station, 78 Arlmont-Harvard Station, 80 Arlington Center-Lechmere, 83 Rindge Avenue-Central Square, 85 Spring Hill-Kendall Square, 87 Arlington Center-Lechmere, 88 Clarendon Hill-Lechmere, 89 Clarendon Hill-Sullivan Square, 91 Sullivan Square-Central Square, 96 Medford Square-Harvard.

SOMERVILLE

Boundaries: North: Medford and the Mystic River. **East:** Charlestown. **South and southwest:** City of Cambridge. **West:** Town of Arlington.

Occupying approximately four square miles west of Charlestown and north of Cambridge, Somerville is the city of seven hills. Although the hills in Somerville aren't as high as those in Beacon Hill, Charlestown, Jamaica Plain and Brookline, they still give the city some geographical variety and contrast. Somerville has a large student population because of its proximity to Harvard and **Tufts University.**

Somerville was included in the original Charlestown land grant of

1630 but became an independent town in 1842 and was upgraded to city status in 1871. Originally used as grazing area for colonial dairy farms, Somerville served as an important military position for the Revolutionary Army. Prospect Hill was the site of military fortifications of which some remnants can still be found in the park. Major General Charles E. Lee used a house on Sycamore Street as his headquarters. General George Washington slept here for at least one night and you could possibly sleep there, too, as it's a four-unit rental building these days.

In the early 19th century Somerville was located right in the northwest transportation corridor from Boston. The city benefited from this by becoming an industrial presence with its brickyards along the Mystic River. By 1842, **Highland Avenue** had become Somerville's civic center (the original Greek Revival City Hall survives) while Union Square became its commercial center. **Bow Street** features many well-preserved period buildings.

As did every other surrounding community, Somerville had its late 19th century building boom when Boston extended the trolley tracks: approximately 50 percent of Somerville's housing was built between 1890 and 1910. Although you will mostly find triple deckers and multiple-family housing in Somerville, you can also find early 20th century brick apartment houses and tenement housing especially on Highland Avenue and around Union Square.

Somerville has several historic districts, including **Spring Hill, Mt. Vernon** and **Westwood Road. Summer Street** is a predominantly Colonial Revival neighborhood with well-preserved Victorian churches. The retail areas around **Davis Square** feature an architecturally important movie theater and an Art Deco bank and diner.

Today Somerville is home to students from both Tufts and Harvard, professionals looking for rental bargains, a large Irish-American and Italian-American population that has lived here for over a century and many immigrants. Somerville has declared itself a politically and socially tolerant haven with no questions asked when it comes to social services. As you can imagine this practice has drawn a lot of fire.

Overall, Somerville apartments are old, large and cheap although they tend to get more expensive the closer you get to Davis Square, the only Somerville square with access to the Red Line. Teale Square and Ball Square are within walking distance to Davis and thus also have higher rents. Winter parking wars are chronic. The Tufts University area is very crowded and parking can be difficult. Often town vs. gown issues become significant in this area as well.

Newcomers may feel uncomfortable in East Somerville because the crime level is perceived to be higher here. Locals define East Somerville as being from the Charlestown border to the McGrath Highway. Newcomers may feel most comfortable in West Somerville, Spring Hill and the western part of the central area.

Following are some descriptions of Somerville's squares.

Union Square, close to Cambridge's Inman Square, is located in a triangular area where Prospect Street, Webster Avenue, Somerville Avenue and Washington Street all cross and intersect. This square has lots of food with many ethnic restaurants including a Portuguese restaurant and bakery. Indian cuisine is well represented here.

Davis Square, located where College Avenue and Highland Street intersect with Holland (which turns into Elm Street), is the only Somerville square on the Red Line. Correspondingly, rents are higher here. Davis Square is close to Cambridge's Porter Square, and it can be hard to figure out where one ends and the other begins. This square hosts an annual Arts Festival each spring and houses many ethnic food markets. The Somerville Theatre shows international shorts and hosts the international animation festival each year. The Baked Bean Theatre provides community theater and comedy shows.

Ball Square is found just past Trum Field on Broadway and houses many bakeries. **Teale Square** is also on Broadway near Powderhouse Boulevard. Teale Square actually borders Route 16 near Arlington. It has restaurants, bars and a grocery store. Davis Square's nightlife spills out toward Teale Square. Both Ball Square and Teale Square are located in the heart of the Tufts zone.

Somerville has a pub on every corner, great pizza places, a large suburban style mall at Assembly Square (near Wellington Fellsway Bridge to Medford), lots of ice cream and a highly Catholic flavor. It is home to the original Bertucci's and the first Steve's Ice Cream. Unfortunately, Somerville is lacking in green space. There are only a few parks but houses often have big backyards and many people have gardens.

Area Code: 617

Zip Codes: West Somerville, 02144; Tufts, 02153; Winter Hill, 02145; Union Square, 02143

Post Offices: Somerville, 237 Washington, 666-0745. West Somerville, 58 Day, 666-0106. Winter Hill, 320 Broadway, 666-5775.

Police: Somerville Police, 220 Washington Street, 625-1600.

Emergency Hospitals: Somerville Hospital, 230 Highland Avenue, 666-4400. Lawrence Memorial, 170 Governors Avenue, Medford, 396-9250. Cambridge Hospital, 1493 Cambridge Street, 498-1000.

Libraries: Main Library, 79 Highland Avenue, 623-5000. West Branch, 40 College Avenue (Davis Square), 623-5000 ext. 2975. East Somerville, 115 Broadway, 623-5000 ext. 2970.

Public School Education: Somerville High, 81 Highland Avenue, 625-6100; Vocational Program, 81 Highland Avenue, 625-6135; Brown Elementary, 201 Willow Avenue, 625-6400; Cummings Elementary, 42 Prescott Street, 625-6430; East Somerville Elementary and Middle, 115 Pearl Street, 625-6500; Edgerly Center K-1, 8 Bonair Street, 625-6340; Healey School West Elementary, Conwell Capen Court, 625-6580; Healey School East Elementary, 8 Butler Drive, 625-6550; Kennedy Elementary-Middle, 85 Elm Street, 625-6600; Lincoln Park Elementary-Middle, 290 Washington Street, 625-6650; Powder House Elementary-Middle, 1060 Broadway, 625-6700; West Somerville Elementary-Middle, 177 Powder House Boulevard, 625-6440; Winter Hill Elementary-Middle, 115 Sycamore Street, 625-6750; Full Circle and Next Wave Schools, 8 Bonair Street, 625-6860.

Public Transportation: Red Line at Davis Square and Porter Square. Buses: 80 Arlington Center-Lechmere, 87 Arlington Center-Lechmere, 88 Clarendon Hill-Lechmere, 89 Clarendon Hill-Sullivan Square, 90 Davis Square-Wellington, 91 Sullivan Square-Central Square, 92 Assembly Square Mall-Downtown, 94 Medford Square-Davis Square, 95 West Medford-Sullivan Square, 96 Medford Square-Harvard, 325 Elm Street, Medford-Haymarket Express, 326 West Medford-Haymarket Express, 353 Burlington Industrial Area-Haymarket Express, 354 Woburn Center-Haymarket or Park Square Express.

ARLINGTON

Boundaries: North: Town of Winchester and Town of Medford. **East:** City of Cambridge and City of Somerville. **South:** Town of Belmont. **West:** Town of Lexington

Arlington is a pretty yet densely populated area. A suburban town on the western perimeter of metro Boston, Arlington covers only four square miles. Not long ago it was profiled in *Boston Magazine* as one of the safest metro Boston neighborhoods.

Originally part of Cambridge, Arlington was first known as Menotomy, then West Cambridge, finally becoming Arlington in 1867. Mass. Ave. and Pleasant, Mystic and Medford Streets are actually native trails adopted as highways in the mid-17th century. The historic "8 Mile Line," a political boundary established in 1636, exists as Warren Street today.

Battle Road is where you will find several colonial houses important for their connection to the Revolutionary War. Arlington also features a wide variety of 19th century housing including Victorian examples along Mass. Ave. and Pleasant Street and workers' cottages along Mill Brook.

As with many of Boston's neighborhoods, Arlington also underwent a building boom in the late 1800s when public transportation was extended to the surrounding communities. This building period produced single family housing with stucco and brick detail and multiple family housing that includes some Art Deco apartments.

Locals segment Arlington into three regions. From East to West they are known as **East Arlington, Arlington Center,** and **Arlington Heights** which borders Lexington. Property values and median incomes rise as you travel west. Arlington Center has architecturally important Neo-Classic civic buildings.

Arlington is relatively affordable and many renters live here. It is less expensive than Belmont and Lexington, but it enjoys the same safe, sleepy, residential reputation. This is a dry town: there are only four existing liquor licenses and they belong to restaurants that seat 100 people. There are no corner bars and no corner cafes to speak of. Although Arlington does have a community theater group and features one of the best movie houses in the area (the Capital Theatre), residents generally head to Cambridge for nightlife and culture.

Shopping is limited but available in Arlington Center. However, there are three malls in the immediate area: Meadow-Glen Mall in Medford, Fresh Pond Mall in Cambridge and Arsenal Mall in Watertown.

Arlington is attractive to young families because it has seven elementary schools. This arrangement means your children will more than likely be able to walk to school. The town also features much open green space for both children and adults to play in: the Arlington Reservoir has an area in which you can swim, Menotomy Rocks Park has some of the most accessible rock climbing around, Minute Man Bike Trail goes right through town, and Spy Pond is a beautiful, deep body of water. An organization called Arlington Recreation offers inexpensive programs and lessons for children and adults.

Public transportation is available in Arlington. The Alewife T Station isn't far, you can grab the Commuter Rail in Belmont and the MBTA (Massachusetts Bay Transit Authority) runs frequent bus routes into Cambridge. Overnight, on-street parking is not allowed in Arlington so make sure your new place includes a parking spot. If you have guests, however, you can call the police department to let them know and your guest won't get a ticket.

Area Code: 781

Zip Codes: 02174, 02175

Post Offices: Arlington Branch, 10 Court Street, 648-1940. Arlington Heights, 1347 Mass. Ave., 643-0201. East Arlington, 240 Mass. Ave., 643-3819.

Police: Community Safety Building, 112 Mystic Avenue, 646-1000.

Emergency Hospitals: Cambridge Hospital, 1493 Cambridge Street, 498-1000. Mt. Auburn Hospital, 330 Mt. Auburn Street, Cambridge, 492-5025. Somerville Hospital, 230 Highland Avenue, Somerville, 666-4400. Symmes Hospital, Hospital Road, Arlington, 646-1500.

Libraries: Robbins/Children's Services, 700 Mass. Ave., 641-4884. Fox Branch, 175 Mass. Ave., 641-5490.

Public School Education: Bishop Elementary, 25 Columbia Road, 641-5400; Brackett Elementary, 66 Eastern Avenue, 641-5407; Dallin Elementary, 185 Florence Avenue, 641-5413; Hardy Elementary, 52 Lake Street, 641-5424; Pierce Elementary, 85 Park Avenue, 641-5446; Stratton Elementary, 180 Mountain Avenue, 641-5453; Thompson Elementary, 60 North Union Street, 641-5467; Ottoson Junior High, 63 Acton Street, 641-5431; Arlington High, 869 Mass. Ave., 646-1000.

Public Transportation: Red Line at Alewife. Commuter Rail at West Medford or Belmont Center. Buses: 62 Bedford VA Hospital-Alewife, 67 Turkey Hills-Alewife, 76 Hanscomb Air Force Base-Alewife, 78 Arlmont-Harvard Station, 79 Arlington Heights-Alewife, 84 Arlmont-Alewife, 350 North Burlington-Alewife.

BELMONT

Boundaries: North: Arlington (coincident with Route 2). **East:** Cambridge (at Fresh Pond). **South:** Watertown (along Belmont Street). **West:** Waltham and Lexington.

The Town of Belmont is a pricey area that is rumored to lead the nation in residents who have won Nobel Prizes. Those who can't find a house to buy in Cambridge often end up in Belmont. Belmont doesn't have the number of rental properties that Arlington and Watertown have, but you can find some if you search diligently along the Watertown border.

Formed from the Cambridge and Watertown land grants in 1859, Belmont's border with Waltham is the original "8 Mile Line" of 1636. Washington Street over Payson Hill to Fresh Pond and Common, School and Grove Streets are all original Native American trails developed into colonial highways.

The streetcar-based building boom in Belmont didn't occur until the early 20th century, resulting in multiple-family housing in the lowlands area (southern part) and single family estates on the high ground. By the middle of the century, Belmont's commercial cores had emerged: **Belmont Center** with a Victorian town hall and depot, **Waverly** (almost in Waltham) which has a Victorian firehouse, and **Cushing Square** which features Revival retail blocks.

Two surviving First Period houses have been preserved on Washington Street. Victorian houses can be found in Belmont Center and Waverly. The Payson Hill area offers examples of Revival styles. And the Presidential area (a neighborhood with streets named after presidents) has many well-kept Colonials.

Belmont views itself as a refuge and likes being publicly defined as boring. It has an excellent school system with well-financed music and athletic departments. Although Belmont has an international population, the town is not diverse racially. It is also not a full-service town: residents go to Cambridge or Boston for nightlife and fine dining.

Many Harvard affiliated people live here and Belmont can be defined as a university and professional bedroom community. It has low-to-no-crime and residents communicate through the Garden Club.

Area Code: 617

Zip Code: 02178

Post Offices: Belmont Post Office, 405 Concord Avenue, 484-4682. Waverly Branch, 492 Trapelo Road, 484-6465.

Police: Belmont Police, 460 Concord Avenue, 484-1215.

Emergency Hospitals: Cambridge Hospital, 1493 Cambridge Street, Cambridge, 498-1000. Mt. Auburn Hospital, 330 Mt. Auburn Street, Cambridge, 492-5025. Symmes Hospital, Hospital Road, Arlington, 646-1500.

Libraries: Main Branch, 336 Concord Avenue, 489-2000. Benton Branch, 75 Oakley, 489-2000. Waverly Branch, 445 Trapelo Road, 489-2000.

Public School Education: Wellington School, 121 Orchard Street, 484-8668; Summer School, 644 Pleasant Street, 484-4110; Belmont Middle and High School, 221 Concord Avenue, 484-4700.

Public Transportation: Commuter Rail at Belmont Center and Waverly. Red Line at Alewife. Buses: 54 Waverly Square-Newton Corner, 73 Waverly Square-Harvard, 74 Belmont Center-Harvard, 76 Hanscomb Air Force Base-Alewife, 78 Arlmont-Harvard Station.

WATERTOWN

Boundaries: North: Town of Belmont. **East:** City of Cambridge. **South:** the Charles River. **West:** Town of Waltham.

Watertown was established in 1630 with a town grant for the Massachusetts Bay Colony. During the next 250 years much land was ceded to surrounding communities (Waltham, Cambridge and Belmont). The town now covers only 4.1 square miles. Except for one small portion set off from Newton early on in its history, Watertown is located on the north shore of the Charles River.

   Watertown Square developed as the town's economic center during Colonial days because of the mills along the river. By the mid-19th century Watertown Square had grown into a large industrial and commercial area because the railroads and streetcars had linked it to Boston. Today, the Square still retains Victorian and Neo-Classic retail blocks.

   During the Federal Period, the Arsenal Street corridor became home to the U.S. arsenal, characterized by brick buildings built through the Civil and First World Wars. Parts of it now comprise the Arsenal Mall. Retail sections of Mt. Auburn Street still have early modern diners and gas stations.

Today Watertown is a residential community with some industry along the Charles River. Many young professionals live along Mt. Auburn Street which has a number of greengrocers and Armenian markets. Watertown has a large population of ethnic groups including Irish, Italian, Greek and Armenian. The town has an Armenian Cultural Center and the locals say that the best breakfasts are served at the Armenian restaurants.

The Oakley Country Club, which borders the Belmont area, has become a desirable place to live. It features brick, stone, clapboard and stucco Colonials, and Victorians with wrap-around porches.

Watertown is greener than many sections of Somerville and Cambridge, bordered by the Mt. Auburn Cemetery on the east and the running paths and MDC facilities along the Charles River. There are playgrounds, tot lots, and an ice skating rink. Housing costs are more affordable than Arlington. Housing stock is mostly multi-family with some apartment complexes and single family houses.

Watertown Square doesn't offer a lot of nightlife, although it does have a few chic restaurants and groovy shops. There are pubs in Orchard Park and on the Waltham and Cambridge borders, but many residents head to Cambridge or Boston for their evening entertainment.

Transportation to and from Watertown is a breeze. Residents have easy access to the Massachusetts Turnpike, Memorial Drive and I-95, as well as express buses to downtown Boston and regular bus service to the Red Line and Cambridge.

Area Code: 617

Zip Code: 02172

Post Offices: Watertown, 126 Main, 924-0081. East Watertown, 589 Mt. Auburn Street, 924-7480.

Police: Watertown Police, 34 Cross Street, 972-6500.

Emergency Hospital: Mt. Auburn Hospital, 330 Mt. Auburn Street, Cambridge, 492-5025.

Libraries: Main Library, 123 Main, 972-6431. East Branch, 481 Mt. Auburn Street, 972-6441. North Branch, Orchard and Waverly Streets, 972-6442. Multi-Service Center, 926-3600.

Public School Education: Coolidge School Special Education, 30 Common Street, 926-7766; Cunniff School, 246 Warren Street, 926-7726; Watertown High, 50 Columbia Avenue, 926-7760;

Watertown Middle School, Waverly Avenue, 926-7783.

Public Transportation: Red Line at Harvard Square. Buses: 70 Cedarwood-Central Square, 70A North Waltham-Central Square, 71 Watertown Square-Harvard, 72 Huron Avenue-Harvard, 73 Waverly Square-Harvard, 74 Belmont Center-Harvard, 78 Arlmont-Harvard Station, 302 Watertown Square-Copley Square Express, 304 Watertown Square-Downtown Express.

WALTHAM

Boundaries: North: Town of Lexington. **East:** Town of Belmont and Town of Watertown. **Southeast:** City of Newton. **Southwest:** Town of Weston. **West:** Town of Lincoln

Waltham, which covers approximately 12 square miles, is located in the westernmost part of metro Boston that is still inside Route 128. It's more rural than Newton but is still a desirable place to live for those who work on "Technology Highway," the section of Route 128 where many computer companies are headquartered. For these reasons, you'll probably have the same problems finding an apartment in Waltham that you would in Newton. This section of the 128 corridor has an extremely low residential vacancy rate.

Waltham was originally a part of Watertown but became an independent town in 1720. Main Street was the post road from Boston and has served as the civic and commercial center of Waltham since the early 18th century. The northern section of Waltham remained agricultural while industry developed along the Charles River in the south. Two rural Federal Period estates survive today: Gore Place and the Vale.

Waltham Center has surviving 19th century factory complexes as well as brick Victorian and Neo-Classic civic and business buildings. The area along Trapelo Road developed as an institutional belt with hospitals located on large landscaped grounds. The castellated college along South Street became Brandeis University with a Victorian cemetery as its neighbor.

The northern section houses a large population of mostly young, educated professionals in expensive condo complexes and exclusive rentals. The southern section is where the action is. Once primarily blue-collar with some Bentley college graduates, this area is slowly gentrifying though the town seems pretty comfortable with this development as rents in the south haven't yet risen to the northern rates. This is also where the community, civic and commercial focus of the town lies.

North Waltham is more affluent with large estates and larger houses and apartment complexes. The large apartment complexes are expensive but private shuttle buses will run you to Alewife T Station and residents feel the swimming pools and tennis courts are worth the price. The Lakeview area (located between Lake Street and the Lexington border) and the Totten Pond Road area have condo complexes and exclusive rentals. This is a youth and/or singles oriented area.

South Waltham is geared toward community, with young families, computer professionals and blue-collar workers. From Beaver Street south to the town line you'll find multiple family housing and complexes that are much more affordable. South Waltham is becoming more racially mixed as the Hispanic, African-American, Indian and Asian populations are on the rise.

Moody Street restaurants are becoming quite popular with waiting lists that Boston eateries would be proud of. Waltham has a lot of shopping: chain stores, clothing stores, huge supermarket, farm stands, and several neighborhood markets. At last count there were 12 hardware stores. You don't have to go far for services.

Waltham has a fair amount of open space but most of it is private. Some public space does exist: City Hall is set on a nice sized common, Lymon Pond has an athletic field and park, Prospect Hill has a ski area and Beaver Brook Reservation is located on the Belmont border.

Waltham is a low crime area and you won't experience the winter parking wars that can rage in Boston, Cambridge and Somerville.

Area Code: 781

Zip Code: 02154

Post Offices: Waltham, 776 Main Street, 893-1100. North Waltham, 846 A Lexington Avenue, 893-5961. South Waltham, 38 Spruce Street, 893-4695.

Police: Waltham Police, 165 Lexington Street, 893-3700.

Emergency Hospital: Waltham/Weston Streets, Hope Avenue, 647-6000

Libraries: Main Library, 735 Main Street, 893-1750.

Public School Education: Banks Elementary, 948 Main Street, 894-8137; Bright Elementary, 260 Grove Street, 647-0347; Fitch Elementary, 10 Ash Street, 891-9173; Fitzgerald Elementary, 140

Beal Road, 891-9772; JFK Junior High, 655 Lexington Street, 891-9319; Macarthur Elementary, 494 Lincoln Street, 891-3896; Northeast Elementary, Putney Lane, 891-4195; South Junior High, 510 Moody, 899-9110; Vocational School, 100 Sumner Street, 647-0309; Whittemore Elementary, 30 Parmenter Road, 891-4548.

Public Transportation: Commuter Rail at Brandeis/Roberts, Waltham Center and Waverly. Buses: 53 Roberts-Newton Corner, 54 Waverly Square-Newton Corner, 56 Waltham Highlands-Newton Corner, 70 Cedarwood-Central Square, 70A North Waltham-Central Square, 305 Waltham Center-Downtown Express.

NEWTON

Boundaries: North, West and South: enclosed by the Charles River. **East:** the Middlesex County line, Brighton, Brookline, West Roxbury.

Newton is a large suburban city comprised of 12 villages that cover 18 square miles of land bordered by the Charles River on three sides. It has a reputation as a pricey place to live which is not surprising since it's relatively crime-free, has abundant green space, lots of shopping, a sense of community and offers access to most of the area's major highways and by-ways (Routes 9 and 1, I-95/128 and the Mass. Turnpike).

The vacancy rate for residential rental properties in this area is very low. It's probably easier to buy a house in Newton than to find an apartment. If you want to live in a Newton village such as Newton Center, Waban, or Chestnut Hill, you'll need to network, use a real estate agent or move somewhere else first while you seek your own path to Newton. The variety of housing is incredible. You'll find Victorian, Colonial, Dutch Colonial, Brick Colonial, Tudor, 19th century workers' housing, Craftsman bungalows and Picturesque Revival.

Newton was originally part of the Cambridge land grant of 1630, incorporating as a separate town in 1688. The **Newton Corner** area was its original settlement. Shortly thereafter mills were established along the falls of the Charles River in what became known as **Newton Upper Falls** and **Newton Lower Falls. Nonantum** also became a site for water power generation.

Newton Centre grew up around the new Meeting House, moved in 1720 from the corner of Cotton and Centre Streets to Newton Centre for accessibility reasons. Railroad extensions in the 1830s were responsible for **Newtonville** and **Auburndale**, villages that began life as railroad depots. Eventually Boston's commuter rail extensions in the late nineteenth century caused the same building boom in Newton that happened everywhere else in the area.

The Charles River Railroad was responsible for the establishment of **Chestnut Hill** (1850s), **Newton Highlands** (1870s) and **Waban** (1880s). **Oak Hill** didn't develop until the 20th century when the wetlands were drained and the automobile was invented. By 1873, Newton had become a city complete with Mayor, Board of Aldermen and Common Council.

Today Newton is an affluent suburban city with a great school system and ethnic diversity. A large Jewish community lives here, so large in fact that the public school system is closed on the first day of Rosh Hashana and on Yom Kippur. All the supermarkets stock necessities for Jewish holy day feasts. There are many active synagogues in Chestnut Hill, Newton Lower Falls, Oak Hill, Newton Centre and Newton Corner. Newton Centre also has a theological seminary and Waban is approximately half-Jewish and half-Catholic.

Nonantum is Newton's own Little Italy. It houses a tight-knit Italian community that celebrates all the festivals. The streets don't have double yellow lines as lane markers, they have red, green and white stripes instead! Nonantum is one of the most affordable neighborhoods in greater Boston. The community is open to non-Italian-Americans and newcomers would feel comfortable in this neighborhood.

The more affordable yet still middle class neighborhoods in Newton are West Newton, Newton Corner, Auburndale and Nonantum. The pricey neighborhoods include Chestnut Hill, Newton Centre, Waban and Newton Highlands. Newton Corner and Chestnut Hill do have high-rise apartments if that's what you're looking for.

Most Newton neighborhoods have all the services you need and usually a good restaurant or pub to boot. Rental bargains may be available but only if you know someone or if you look really hard.

Public transportation is Boston-centric. You won't have any trouble getting to downtown Boston, but there are no cross-Newton buses to speak of.

Newton's green space is abundant. The area has large yards and cemeteries, at least four country clubs, the Charles River to the north, west and south, and many city parks.

Area Code: 617

Zip Codes: Chestnut Hill, 02167; Newton, 02158; Newtonville,

02160; West Newton, 02165; Newton Centre, 02159; Newton Lower Falls, 02162; Newton Highlands, 02167; Newton Upper Falls, 02164; Waban, 02168; Auburndale, 02166

Post Offices: Boston College, 140 Commonwealth Avenue, 552-3522. Chestnut Hill, 12 Middlesex Road, 566-7984. Newtonville, 897 Washington Street, 244-6233. West Newton, 525 Waltham Street, 244-7277. Newton Centre, 211 Sumner Street, 244-2062. Newton Lower Falls, 2344 Washington Street, 527-4045. Newton Upper Falls, 77 Oak Street, 527-2491. Newton Highlands, 63 Lincoln Street, 527-0748. Waban, 83 Wyman Street, 527-7289. Auburndale, 2122 Commonwealth Avenue, 527-8529. Nonantum, 326 Watertown Street, 244-1073.

Police: Newton Police, 1321 Washington Street, 522-7240.

Emergency Hospital: Newton-Wellesley, 2014 Washington Street, 243-6000.

Libraries: Main, 300 Homer Street, 552-7162. Auburndale, 375 Auburn Street, 552-7158. Corner Branch, 125 Vernon Street, 552-7157. Nonantum, 144 Bridge Street, 552-7163. Waban, 1608 Beacon Street, 552-7166.

Public School Education: Angler Elementary, 1697 Beacon Street, 552-7350; Bigelow Middle School, 42 Vernon Street, 552-7800; Bowen Elementary, 280 Cypress Street, 552-7361; Brown Junior High, 125 Meadowbrook Road, 552-7409; Burr Elementary, 171 Pine Street, 552-7364; Cobol Elementary, 229 Cabot Street, 552-7369; Countryside Elementary, 191 Dedham Street, 552-7373; Day Junior High, 21 Minot Place, 552-7379; Franklin Elementary, 125 Derby Street, 552-7389; Horace Mann School, 687 Watertown Street, 552-7403; Lincoln-Eliot, 191 Pearl Street, 552-7400; Mason-Rice, 149 Pleasant Street, 552-7406; Spaulding Memorial, 250 Brookline Street, 552-7561; Newton North High, 360 Lowell Street, 552-7422; Newton South High, 140 Brandeis Road, 552-7515.

Public Transportation: Green Line, Riverside. Commuter Rail at Auburndale, West Newton, and Newtonville. Buses: 52 Dedham Mass/Charles River-Watertown Square, 58 Auburndale-Newton Corner, 59 Needham Junction-Watertown Square, 300 Riverside-Downtown Express, 301 Brighton Center-Downtown Express, 302 Watertown Square-Copley Express, 304A Newton Corner-Downtown Express, 305 Waltham Center-Downtown Express.

BROOKLINE

Boundaries: North: just south of Commonwealth Avenue, Boston. **East:** the west side of the Riverway and Jamaicaway, Boston. Boundary then jags west to St. Paul's Avenue on the west side of Jamaica Pond. **South:** Norfolk and Middlesex County line, Newton. **West:** Allston-Brighton.

Brookline is a separate town that occupies about six square miles in the center of western Boston. Surrounded by Boston on all sides except the south, its residents see it as an oasis within Boston. It is a beautiful town with lots of green space and a confusing street layout in its southern areas. Rents and property taxes are high but residents feel that the town services (police and schools) are worth it. There is absolutely no overnight on-street parking for any reason in Brookline, not even for guests, and parking spaces increase the amount you pay for rent.

Originally a part of Boston, Brookline became an independent entity in 1705 with the Charles River marking its northern division from Cambridge. Over the years Brookline annexed the Pill Hill area from Boston as Boston annexed from Brookline the Charles River tidal flats along Commonwealth Avenue in order to connect Brighton to Boston.

Brookline's economy remained agricultural until the Federal Period when residential development began. With the mid-19th century streetcar expansion came another building boom for Brookline. Brookline Village developed into Picturesque (an architectural style) subdivisions and the Longwood area adopted early Gothic style stone houses and churches.

Coolidge Corner went through its developmental boom during the early 20th century. It was built up with brick and faced stone apartments along Beacon Street and Commonwealth Ave. while high density blocks were built on Aspinwall Hill. You'll find triple deckers along Cypress/Boylston as well as large Revival style synagogues on Fisher Hill.

Brookline has three major commercial centers whose names are also used to designate neighborhoods. **Brookline Village** is located at the intersection of Boylston and Harvard and extends up Washington. This neighborhood is the civic center of Brookline: the fire department, police station, high school and municipal court are all located in this area. Brookline Village has many interesting shops and boutiques. **Washington Square** is located at the corner of Washington and Beacon Streets. This neighborhood has great places to lunch, dine, get coffee and shop. Coolidge Corner is located at the corner of Beacon and Harvard Streets. It features a major shopping and dining district with a movie theater offering a variety of films, kosher and non-kosher restaurants, bookstores, clothing stores and coffee shops.

The **Longwood** area borders Boston's Roxbury Crossing where the medical area is located. Many medical students and workers try to find housing in the area around Aspinwall and Longwood Avenues. The Westbrook Village area is in the southwest corner of Brookline. This area is gorgeous but doesn't feature any rental properties.

The town of Brookline is home to a thriving Jewish community. Harvard Street is lined with kosher delis, bakeries and bagel shops and also features a few Israeli import shops. Brookline actually has two kosher Chinese restaurants and a kosher Chinese caterer. However, although the Jewish population lends continuity and community to Brookline, many non-Jews live here too. It's very convenient for students.

Brookline has seen a number of Jewish migrations to its tree-lined streets. Early on, the neighborhood was home to German Jews. Then in the 1930s through the 1960s a large number of Eastern European Jewish families found Brookline after having first settled in Dorchester, Roxbury and Mattapan. Most recently, Russian Jews have made Brookline their home. A small Sephardic community can also be found here.

Brookline is clean, accessible and relatively crime free. It is home to Brookline Adult and Community Education, the largest public education program in Massachusetts.

Area Code: 617

Zip Code: 02146

Post Offices: Brookline, 1295 Beacon Street, 738-1776.

Police: Brookline Village, 207 Washington Street, 566-7465; also 350 Washington Street, 730-2248.

Emergency Hospitals: Beth Israel Hospital, 330 Brookline Avenue, Boston, 735-5397. Children's Hospital, 300 Longwood Avenue, Boston, 735-6624. St. Elizabeth's Hospital, 736 Cambridge Street, Boston, 789-3000.

Libraries: Main Library, 361 Washington Street, 730-2345. Coolidge Corner Branch, 31 Pleasant Street, 730-2380. Putterham Branch, 959 West Roxbury Parkway, 730-2385.

Public School Education: Baker Elementary, 205 Beverly Road, 730-2510; Driscoll Elementary, 64 Westbourne Terrace, 730-2530; Devotion Elementary, 345 Harvard Street, 730-2520; Heath

Elementary, 100 Elliot Street , 730-2540; Lawrence Elementary, 27 Frances Street, 730-2550; Lincoln School, 19 Kennard Street, 730-2560; Pierce Elementary, 50 School Street, 730-2580; Rinckle School, 50 Druce Street, 730-2590; Brookline High, 115 Greenough, 730-2603.

Public Transportation: The Green Line. Buses: 51 Cleveland Circle-Forest Hills, 60 Chestnut Hill-Kenmore, 65 Brighton Center-Kenmore, 66 Harvard Square-Dudley Square.

MEDFORD

Boundaries: East: Everett and Malden. **South:** Somerville. **West:** Mystic Valley Parkway. **Northwest:** Bord Road, Elm Street, East Bord Road, Winchester.

Located five miles northwest of Boston off Interstate 93, Medford is home to another esteemed Boston-area university, Tufts. The university adds ethnic diversity to the city's population of 56,000.

In pre-Colonial times, Medford was home to the Pawtucket Indians. A monument is erected to Sagamore John and his followers in Sagamore Park in West Medford.

During much of the 17th century the area was a great plantation deeded to Matthew Craddock, a London merchant, Puritan and governor. This land became Medford, first as a town in 1695 and eventually a city in 1892.

Medford's early commerce relied heavily on its tidewater seaport, as well as shipbuilding and distilling. Irish immigrants staffed local brick-yards and the Medford granite quarry. With the decline of shipbuilding, the city's businesses expanded into textiles, shoe-making machinery, chemicals and even to brass soda fountain manufacturing.

The city has a strong connection with nature. The Middlesex Fells Reservation, which was a source of timber during the early shipbuilding era, offers more than 2,000 acres of forest close to Boston (contact the Friends of the Middlesex Fells Reservation 662-2340). There is also fresh water fishing, hiking, nature observing, sightseeing, and walking and jogging paths in the Mystic River Reserve. Also, Tufts offers such facilities as baseball, softball, football, and soccer fields, tennis courts, hiking paths and ice skating.

Medford has a rich architectural past, including the Isaac Royall estate, and Federal, Greek Revival and Victorian buildings. The city's neighborhoods have tree-lined streets, ranging from older two and three-family homes in South Medford to newer homes in West Medford off High Street. Other neighborhoods include Wellington, Fulton Heights, Lawrence Estates and Medford Hillside.

Medford's shopping areas include Salem Street, Main Street, Riverside Avenue and High Street in Medford Square and West Medford. There is also the Meadow Glen Mall along the Mystic River on Route 16.

Area Code: 781

Zip Codes: 02155, 02153 (P.O. boxes at Tufts University) and 02156 (P.O. boxes in West Medford)

Post Offices: Central Post Office, 20 Forest Street, 396-6763. Tufts University branch, 470 Boston Avenue, 627-3495. West Medford branch, 485 High Street, 483-8967.

Police: Medford Police, 100 Main Street, 395-1212 (emergency), 391-6404 (business). State Police, 520 Fellsway, 396-0100.

Emergency Hospitals: Lawrence Memorial Hospital of Medford, 170 Governors Avenue, 396-9250. Tufts University Health Service, 124 Professors Row, 627-3350.

Libraries: Medford Public Library, 111 High Street, 395-7950.

Public School Education: Brooks Elementary, 388 High Street, 393-2228; Columbus School, 37 Hicks Avenue, 393-2230; Dame School, 80 George Street, 393-2234; Davenport School, 25 Horne Avenue, 393-2236; Forest Park School, 225 Governors Avenue, 393-2238; Franklin School, 68 Central Avenue, 393-2238; Gleason School, 160 Playstead Road, 393-2244; Hervey School, 122 Sharon, 393-2248; Kennedy School, 215 Harvard Street, 393-2349; Osgood School, 101 Fourth Street, 393-2333; Swan School, 75 Park, 393-2340; Curtis/Tufts Alternative High School, 437 Main Street, 393-2343; Hillside School, 15 Capen Street, 393-2250; Hobbs Junior High, 25 Auburn Street, 393-2347; Roberts Junior High, 35 Court Street, 393-2336; Lincoln Junior High, 251 Harvard Street, 393-2327; Medford High, 489 Winthrop Street, 393-2325.

Public Transportation: Commuter rail from West Medford to North Station, Boston. Travel time is 11-12 minutes. There are 30 parking spaces at the MBTA station. The Orange Line from

Wellington Station, 11 minutes to Downtown Crossing, Boston. 1,253 parking spaces. Bus service is available only within Medford from the Malden Transportation Center off the Orange Line. Buses: 80 Medford-Cambridge-Arlington, 90 Medford-Somerville, 94 Medford-Somerville, 95 Medford-Charlestown, 96 Medford-Somerville-Cambridge, 97 Medford-Everett-Malden, 99 Medford-Everett-Malden, 100 Wellington Station via Fellsway, 101 Malden-Medford-Somerville-Charlestown, 106 Medford-Everett-Malden, 108 Linden Square, 110 Medford-Everett-Revere, 112 Medford-Everett-Chelsea-East Boston, 134 North Woburn, 325 Medford-Charlestown-Boston, 326 Medford-Charlestown-Boston.

QUINCY

Boundaries: North: Dorchester Bay. South: Route 3A, Braintree. **West:** Blue Hills Reservation, Interstate 93, the Southeast Expressway. **East:** Quincy Bay.

Quincy is known as the "City of Presidents," having served as home to the second and sixth presidents, John Adams and John Quincy Adams, as well as John Hancock.

While the city was once considered an Italian-American and Irish-American enclave, the demographics are beginning to change. There is an increasing number of Asian-American and African-American families among the city's 90,000 residents.

Quincy is located between the Blue Hills and Quincy Bay, about seven miles south of Boston. Once known as a center for shipbuilding, the city's waterfront offers a beautiful view of the islands of Boston Harbor as well as the Boston skyline just to the north.

Although the Quincy Shipyard closed in 1986, there is a renewed effort to revive shipbuilding in the Fore River area. Military enthusiasts can get a glimpse of one of the great warships, the USS Salem, a decommissioned heavy cruiser now anchored at the U.S. Naval Shipbuilding Museum (479-7900) near the Fore River Bridge.

Route 3A serves as a main link to Boston, resulting in heavy traffic to and from Boston during the morning and evening rush hours. But the auto flow should ease when the Old Colony Rail expansion project is completed, with a main commuter rail station located in Quincy Center.

The rail project and Central Artery Project should actually help in the continued conversion of Quincy from a bedroom community for workers headed to Boston to a growing destination to work. The MBTA Red Line has four major stations with large parking areas: the Quincy Adams station with 2,200 parking spaces, Quincy Center with 870 parking spaces, Wollaston with 522 parking spaces, and North Quincy with 587 parking spaces.

Neighborhoods include **Quincy Point, South Quincy, West Quincy, Quincy Center, Presidents Hill, Merrymount, Adams Shore, Germantown, Hough's Neck** (pronounced Howe's), **Wollaston Hill, Wollaston, Montclair, Atlantic, North Quincy, Squantum** and **Marina Bay**.

Pricier places to buy a home include Presidents Hill, Furnace Brook Parkway/Adams Street in West Quincy, Wollaston Hill, Squantum, Marina Bay and Governor's Road in West Quincy.

By the way, unlike the other 19 cities and towns around the U.S. that are also named Quincy, the way to pronounce this Quincy is "Quin-zee." That's because the original Quincy family which settled here at Mount Wollaston pronounced it with a "z" rather than a "c" including Colonel John Qincy, the city's namesake and grandfather of John Adams.

Area code: 617

Zip Codes: Much of Quincy, 02169; Wollaston, 02170; North Quincy, Squantum and Marina Bay

Post Offices: Quincy, 47 Washington Street, 02169, 773-0568; North Quincy, 454 Hancock Street, 02171, 328-5544; Wollaston, 5 Beach Street, 472-7193, 02170.

Police: Police Headquarters, 1 Sea Street, 479-1212.

Emergency Hospital: Quincy Hospital, 114 Whitwell Street, 773-6100.

Libraries: Thomas Crane Public Library, 40 Washington Street, 376-1300; Adams Shore branch, 519 Sea Street, 376-1325; North Quincy branch, 381 Hancock Street, 376-1320; Wallaston branch, 41 Beale Street, 376-1330.

Public School Education: Beechwood Knoll School, 225 Fenno Street, 984-8781; Bernazzani Elementary, 701 Furnace Brook Parkway, 984-8713; Hough Atherton Elementary, 1084 Sea Street, 984-8797; Lincoln Hancock, 300 Granite Street, 984-8715; Merrymount, 4 Agawam Road 984-8762; Montclair, 8 Belmont Street, 984-8708; Parker, 148 Billings Road 984-8710; Point-

Webster, Lancaster Street. 984-8721; Snug Harbor, Palmer Street, 984-8763; Squantum, 50 Huckins Avenue 984-8706; Wollaston School 205 Beale Street, 984-8791; Atlantic Middle School, 86 Hollis Avenue, 984-8727; Broad Meadows Middle School, 50 Calvin Road 984-8723; Central Middle School, 1012 Hancock Street, 984-8725; Sterling Middle School, 444 Granite Street, 984-8729; Quincy North High, 318 Hancock Street, 984-8745; Quincy High, 52 Coddington Street, 984-8754.

Transportation: There is a Quincy stop on the newly-built Old Colony commuter rail line. The Red Line. Harbor Express Boats run to Boston and Logan Airport. Buses: 210 Quincy-Dorchester-Boston, 211 Squantum, 212 North Quincy Station, 214 Germantown, 215 Ashmont, 216 Houghs Neck, 217 Quincy-Milton-Dorchester-Boston via Wollaston Beach, 220/221 Quincy-Hingham-Weymouth, 222 Quincy-Hingham-East Weymouth, 225 Quincy-Brantree-Weymouth Landing, 230 Quincy-Braintree-Holbrook-Brockton, 236 Quincy-Braintree, 238 Quincy-Braintree-Randolph-Dorchester-Boston, 240 Quincy-Braintree-Randolph-Avon-Dorchester-Boston, 245 Quincy-Milton-Dorchester-Boston, 276 Quincy-Boston express.

OTHER NEIGHBORHOODS

There are a number of Boston neighborhoods missing from this guide because of newcomer comfort issues: real or perceived crime, accessibility, and/or the tight-knit local community factor that can make newcomers feel like outsiders.

South Boston, Roxbury and Mattapan all have much to offer. For example, South Boston is reaping the benefits of the harbor cleanup and other city-sponsored development projects. However, we've tried to identify neighborhoods in which newcomers will find an immediate comfort level. Once you've lived in the area for a while, your attitudes may change and you're likely to explore the rest of Boston.

ADDITIONAL AREAS

Many people live in the surrounding suburban areas. Here are a few places to check into if you don't mind a longer commute. Some of these towns are on the Commuter Line and it would be possible to use public transportation from them.

West: Bedford, Concord, Framingham, Lexington, Lincoln, Natick, Needham, Wellesley, Weston, Winchester, Woburn.

North Shore: Beverly, Danvers, Lynn, Marblehead, Malden, Peabody, Revere, Salem, Saugus, Swampscott.

South Shore: Braintree, Cohasset, Weymouth, Hingham, Scituate. Braintree is on both the Red Line and the Commuter Line.

BOSTON ADDRESS LOCATOR

You *will* get lost in Boston. Often. However, getting lost will give you an opportunity to learn about your new city. And you should never feel embarrassed about being lost here because even people who have lived in Boston for years get lost on occasion. One of the city's nicknames is the Hub and it's called that for a reason. Streets are circular. There's a story about how the streets of Boston are built on old cow trails and it's probably true. Boston streets pre-date the many local landfill projects and the streets often had to circle around salt marshes or tidal flats. The only grid-like sections of Boston belong to Back Bay and South End, real estate produced by landfill projects of epic proportions during the 19th century.

A standard address locator that explains how the grid works just isn't possible for Boston. Instead, we offer the following tips:

- Get a good map. Never use a transit map for directions.
- Boston is relatively small. If you're lost, first find out what town you're in because you may have left the city limits without realizing it.
- When people tell you something is "on massave" they're really saying it's "on Mass. Ave." which is short for Massachusetts Avenue; and, similarly, when people tell you something is "on commave" they're really saying it's "on Comm. Ave." which is short for Commonwealth Avenue.
- Learn the names and locations of all the squares because all things are located in relation to the nearest square. By the way, squares are usually (but not always) triangular.

• Most towns and cities have streets with the same names. When look-ing for an address make sure you know which city the street belongs to. Some common street names for all the surrounding communities are Broadway, Cambridge, Harvard, Washington, and many more.

Here's a list of major streets that run through more than one com-munity. Get to know this list because as streets pass from town to town the numbering system changes. Make sure you're certain which town the address belongs to.

Massachusetts Avenue (always referred to as Mass. Ave.)
Commonwealth Avenue (always referred to as Comm. Ave.)
Beacon Street
Boylston Street
Washington Street
Pleasant Street

Sometimes streets change names at town borders. Sometimes streets change names for no apparent reason. For example as you drive south on the Fence it becomes the Riverway then the Jamaicaway then the Arborway. Sometimes streets disappear and reappear — Boylston, for example.

Also, become familiar with an old New England traffic institution called the "rotary," "roundabout" or "traffic circle." You may find your-self lost after you've encountered one. This is because you got off the cir-cle in the wrong place. Turn around and try it again.

Once you've learned your way around Boston you'll be bored by cities with grid systems!

APARTMENT HUNTING

Since the mid-1990s, the Boston-area residential real estate market has been extraordinarily strong. Vacancy rates in Boston are at historic lows (though there is some seasonal variation in the trend due to the thousands of students who flow in and out of the city each year). Generally, however, vacancies don't stay available long, and those that do tend to be expensive. Whether or not the price of apartments shock you will depend to some extent on where you're from. Newcomers from the Midwest or the South will probably feel prices are high. Those from New York and California should experience little or no sticker shock.

Don't despair, however. Salaries, like real estate prices, are generally higher in Boston than in many other parts of the country. In addition, with a combination of perseverance, information and realism, it *is* possible to find a reasonable and relatively affordable apartment in Boston, you just have to know where to look (or not look). For example, historic and scenic neighborhoods such as Beacon Hill and Back Bay are among the most expensive places in which to rent, followed by such areas as Allston/Brighton, Fenway/Longwood, Dorchester and Mattapan.

First, decide how much you can afford to spend on rent (if you're **looking to buy** skip to the House/Condo Hunting section below). To gauge your price range, plan on spending no more than 25 to 30 percent of your monthly income on rent. Next, figure out your space needs and whether or not you want to live alone. Finally, pick a few target neighborhoods. To help you in this important task, get as much information as you can by reading this book, asking friends and co-workers about where they live, and if possible, taking a tour of the city's neighborhoods. Then start to home in on where you think you may want to live.

Keep in mind that Boston has its share of high-rises but if you have an aversion to large apartment buildings, fear not — two and three family dwellings are also abundant. While choosing your perfect neighborhood, you also have a wide variety of architectural styles to choose from: late

Georgian, Federal, Greek Revival, Gothic Revival (Early, Carpenter, High Victorian), French and English Victorian, triple deckers (Queen Anne and Colonial Revival), Italianate, Mansard, Philadelphia, brownstone and brick rowhouses, Colonial — the list is almost endless.

Apart from Beacon Hill, Back Bay, South End and parts of Charlestown, apartments in Boston are large. Granted, quarters in the so-called "student slums" may be tiny and many beautiful examples of Victorian architecture have been chopped into efficiency and one bedroom apartments. But a typical triple decker in Brighton, Jamaica Plain or Somerville has three bedrooms and a foyer. Many have front and back porches.

Realize that there are enough people apartment hunting in Boston at any time to make it necessary to travel with your checkbook. If you find what you're looking for in the neighborhood you want to live in, *take it!* Be prepared to spend some time looking.

Note that Boston landlords are not required to supply you with a refrigerator. Find out who owns the refrigerator before you assume the apartment is equipped with one.

If you prefer character over modern convenience and efficiency, keep in mind that it may cost you. That gorgeous, spacious apartment in a Queen Anne triple-decker may give you a heart attack when you get your first heating bill. If the apartment has gas or electric heat you can call Boston Edison or Boston Gas (or the appropriate utility in the surrounding cities and towns) to find out the unit's average monthly bills. However, many buildings are still heated with oil and there is no regulated oil utility in the oil distribution industry. If the apartment has oil heat you'll have to ask your potential landlord and neighbors about heating costs during the winter months.

Many apartments turn over in August/September because a sizeable portion of the rental market serves the student population. Still, if you can avoid it, don't apartment hunt in August. Boston's summers are sticky and hot which translates into frequent "bad air days." Apartment hunting in 95 degree weather while gasping for breath is not a pleasant experience and may even result in a hasty decision.

Boston and suburban police can supply you with safety information about a specific neighborhood, square, street, etc. Call the Community Officer in your precinct (see the Neighborhood profiles for these numbers) with questions about a prospective neighborhood and information about local crime watch organizations.

Here are some specific ways to find your new home.

NEWSPAPER CLASSIFIED ADVERTISEMENTS

- *The Boston Globe* (www.boston.com), especially the Sunday *Globe*, for over-all Boston area listings.
- *The Boston Herald* (www.bostonherald.com) puts out a thorough listing on Saturday.
- *The Phoenix* (www.bostonphoenix.com) for greater Boston area rentals, ads for sublets and shares.
- *The Tab* (www.townonline.com) for Boston area listings.
- *The Newton Graphic* for Newton rentals.
- You may also find listings in the *Somerville Journal, Cambridge Chronicle, Jamaica Plain Citizen, Allston-Brighton Journal, Brookline Citizen, Watertown Press, West Roxbury Transcript, South End News.*

RENTAL AGENTS

Many landlords list their apartments with rental agents. If you're in a hurry to find a place to live, a rental service may be the only way to do so. And it can be the only way you find an apartment in particularly popular areas such as the mid-Route 128 region. The catch: you pay the finder's fee which is often 50% of one month's rent.

If you decide to use an agent, try to get a recommendation from someone familiar with the neighborhood that you want to live in. There are professional rental agents and there are fast-buck operators. Again, get a reference.

Rental offices are so plentiful that you almost can't walk down the street, any street, without seeing one. There are also free "weekly shopper" type rental listing publications at most bus stops and street corners. You'll find them with the newspaper machines and you can always look through them and gather names from appealing listings. The neighborhood you found the publication in will be prominently featured so if you're interested in a specific neighborhood, check out the freebie rental publications on its streets.

Be specific about your price range and the neighborhood you're interested in. Good brokers won't waste your time taking you to an apartment that doesn't meet your needs because that's the one they want to rent to you. If your broker takes you to see apartments that don't fit your needs, find someone else.

Pay attention to the way the broker treats the current residents if the apartment is still inhabited. Did the broker call and get permission before taking you to see it? Once you were at the building, did the broker ring from the lobby or did s/he let him or herself in the front entrance and then knock on the apartment door? If a broker walks in on tenants who didn't answer the door because they were in the shower, take notice: if it happens to the current tenants it will happen to you.

Using a broker may save you time and energy but you may need to spend some time locating one you feel comfortable with. The following list offers a few places to start your search.

- **Back Bay**
  Cabot & Company, 213 Newbury Street, Boston, 262-6200 (e-mail: cabotcore@aol.com)
  Prudential Gibson, 227 Newbury Street, Boston, 375-6900
- **Beacon Hill**
  Otis & Ahearne, 81 Newbury Street, Boston, 267-3500
- **Charlestown**
  Gibson Real Estate, 142 Main Street, Charlestown, 242-3073
- **South End**
  Prudential Gibson, 556 Tremont Street, Boston, 426-6900
- **Jamaica Plain**
  Pleasant Realty, 713 Centre Street, Jamaica Plain, 522-4600
  (www.pleasantrealty.com)
- **Arlington, Belmont, Watertown**
  Real Estate 109, 459 Common Street, Belmont, 489-5110
- **Brookline**
  Chobee Hoy Associates, 18 Harvard Street, Brookline Village, 739-0067
  (e-mail: homeahoy@chobeehoy.com)
- **Cambridge**
  DeWolfe New England, 171 Huron Avenue, Cambridge, 864-8566
  (www.dewolfenewengland.com)
- **Medford**
  Century 21 Advanced Realty, 284 Salem Street, Medford, 781-395-2121
  (www.c21advanced.com)
- **Newton**
  Century 21 Garden City, 324 Walnut Street, Newton, 969-2121
  (www.newtoncentury21.com)
- **Quincy**
  Century 21 Annex Realty, 49 Beale Street, Quincy, 472-4330

- **Somerville**
Bremis Realty, 1177 Broadway, Somerville, 623-2500
- **Waltham**
Justin Reynolds, 5 Banks Street, Waltham, 781-899-2003

DIRECT ACTION

Check the **bulletin boards** in neighborhood cafes, ice cream shops, grocery stores and laundromats. If you're associated with a university or college, check the housing office or the school's web site. Flyers for apartments can often be found on bulletin boards in university areas.

Hit the streets. Drive, walk or bike through prospective neighborhoods and look for "For Rent" signs. Many landlords, particularly the smaller ones, don't use classifieds at all.

Even if you don't see a "For Rent" sign, if you see a building that you're interested go ahead and **call the managing agent.** The phone number is usually displayed quite prominently. If it isn't, look in the phone book.

INTERNET

The internet offers a wealth of information to those with the time to sift through much online dross. Do a search on one of the popular "search-engines" or try these two sites out for starters:

- **The Roommate Connection** (www.dwellingsma.com/)
- **Boston Apartment Online Rental Magazine** (www.bostonapartments.com/bahome.html)

TEMPORARY HOUSING ARRANGEMENTS

If you still need time to find the right place, consider a **short term sublet**. Many students leave in the beginning of the summer when they still have two or three months left on a lease. May and June are the best times to find these arrangements. Check the *Phoenix* and the *Tab*.

You could also try a YMCA or a YWCA. A few are listed in the Temporary Lodgings chapter near the end of this guide. The Temporary Lodgings chapter also contains a list of other inexpensive lodging options for you.

LEASES AND SECURITY DEPOSITS

If you're moving to the Boston area from out of state, it makes sense to find out what your rights are as a tenant in Massachusetts. Fortunately, there are a couple of good resources available for you.

Tenant's Commandments, a pamphlet that describes tenants rights, is available from the Massachusetts Executive Office of Consumer Affairs and Business Regulation. This office is located at 1 Ashburton Place, 14th Floor, Room 1411, Boston, 02108 or call them at 727-7780.

You can pick up the *Renter's Rights, A Guide for Massachusetts Tenants* by Paul Sandburg for $5.95 at most bookstores. A thorough publication called *Legal Tactics: Self-Defense for Tenants in Massachusetts* is produced by the Massachusetts Law Reform Institute (69 Canal Street, Boston, 02114). It costs $15. You can also order it through Massachusetts Continuing Legal Education (10 Winter Place, Boston 02108, 482-2205).

Landlords and rental agents usually seem nice while they're showing you the apartment. However, they make their living by renting apartments, so naturally your interactions before signing your lease will most likely be pleasant ones. Most important is what happens after you move in. Be informed and protect yourself.

LEASES

Always read a lease carefully. Many landlords use standard forms and standard forms are typically weighted in favor of landlords. However, you can negotiate with your landlord, striking out some things and adding others which will make signing the lease more comfortable psychologically. Typical issues include sublet restrictions and pet clauses.

Some leases contain illegal clauses — but don't worry. You can't sign away your rights. If there is an illegal clause you can't be forced to comply with it. For example, residential landlords are required to pay for water and sewage. A lease requiring the tenant to pay for this utility cannot be enforced. Furthermore, tenants must agree in writing to pay for the fuel to heat the water. If this clause is not included in the lease, the landlord is responsible for heating your water as well.

Valid leases in Massachusetts include the following:

- The amount of rent,
- The date on which your tenancy begins and ends,
- The amount of your security deposit and your rights concerning it,

- The names, addresses and phone numbers of your landlord and any other person responsible for maintaining the property; and
- The person authorized to receive notices and court papers.

Make sure you get all promises not included on the lease in writing. If you can't get additional promises in writing you should at least have a witness who isn't your roommate or family member. Finally, make sure you can prove the state of your apartment when you moved in (take photographs or a video). This could save you in case the landlord makes unjustifiable deductions from your security deposit to cover repairs.

SECURITY DEPOSITS

The most your landlord can legally charge you when you move in is the first month's rent, last month's rent, a security deposit of one month's rent, and the cost of a new lock. However, landlords usually ask for a security deposit of one month's rent and rarely ask for first and last month's rent. Needless to say, always get a receipt for any money you pay to a landlord.

In Massachusetts, security deposits must be deposited in interest-bearing accounts. Your landlord must pay you annual interest at the end of each year of tenancy and within thirty days of moving out. Security deposits must be returned within thirty days after the tenancy ends. Landlords may deduct the reasonable cost of repairs for damage caused by the tenant *but* normal wear and tear expenses are *not* deductible. If your landlord does not return your deposit within thirty days you can sue for up to three times the amount of the deposit plus court costs and attorney fees.

Be aware that some landlords tack on bogus fees such as "rental fees," "pet fees," "fees for credit checks" or "holding deposits." These are illegal. If you choose to pay them rather than lose the apartment, consider subtracting the charges from your future rent payments.

When you pay the last month's rent in advance, use that money as the last month's rent because you won't get it back. The last month's rent is not a security deposit. However, the landlord must still pay interest on it.

RENT CONTROL

In 1994, rent control was prohibited by a state-wide ballot. Instead, the

Boston Rent Equity Board now provides mediation between landlords and tenants, legal advice for both landlords and tenants, and assistance in housing placement for elderly, handicapped, or low-income residents.

- **Boston Rent Equity Board** - Boston City Hall, Room 709, Boston 02201, 635-4200

TENANT RIGHTS ORGANIZATIONS

Massachusetts does provide substantial legal protection for tenants. Following are some organizations that can offer you more information about your rights and can help if you have a dispute with your landlord.

- **Action for Boston Community Development** - 178 Tremont Street, 7th Floor, Boston 02111, 357-6000 (www.bostonabcd.org)
- **Cambridge Economic Opportunity Committee, Inc.** - 11 Inman Street, Cambridge 02139, 868-2900
- **Community Action Agency of Somerville** - 66-70 Union Square #104, Somerville 02143, 623-7370
- **Massachusetts Tenants Organization** - 14 Beacon Street, Room 808, Boston 02108, 367-6260
- **Tenant Advocacy Project** - Harvard Law School, Austin Hall, Room 202, Cambridge 02138, 495-4394

Boston tenants (Boston, Charlestown, Jamaica Plain, Allston/ Brighton, Roslindale, West Roxbury, etc.) with emergency landlord problems (e.g. no heat or threatened lockout) can call the Mayor's hotline for intervention. This line is open seven days a week:

- **Mayor's 24-Hour Hotline**, Mayor's Office of Constituent Services - 635-4500.

RENTER'S INSURANCE

Renter's insurance is a good idea, and since you're only insuring your possessions, not the structure, it's usually quite affordable. Generally, renter's insurance will protect you in the event of a whole host of catastrophes, including theft and water damage. Before you get a policy it may be a good idea to get a copy of the pamphlet *Insuring Your Home: A Consumer Guide for Owners and Renters* from the Massachusetts Division of

Insurance, 521-7777.

You can get renter's insurance directly through your insurance agent or you can take care of it yourself by applying directly to **FAIR Plan.** You'll need the standard property insurance form Homeowners 4 Contents Broad Form (HO4) which you can get at any insurance office. FAIR Plan is located at 2 Center Plaza in Boston across from City Hall Plaza, 723-3800, and is open from 8:00 a.m. to 4:00 p.m.

HOUSE/CONDO HUNTING

If you're ready to put your money down in the Boston area and become an owner, here are a few tips:

• Early in the process, check out your credit reports. They are free to anyone denied credit, insurance or a job within the past 60 days; otherwise, they cost $8. Contact: Equifax (800-685-1111), Experian (888-397-3742) and Trans Union (800-888-4213 or 800-916-8800). It's best to get a copy from each service because each company's report is usually different. If you discover some inaccuracy in a report with your name on it, you should write to the service immediately and request that it be corrected. By law they must respond to your request within 30 days. If you are insecure about your credit record, before you apply for a mortgage, call Fannie Mae's nonprofit credit counseling service at 800-732-6643.

• Regarding how much you will have to borrow, keep in mind the following rule of thumb: lenders will probably be reluctant to give you a loan that is more than 28% of your pre-tax income.

• When calculating your budget, don't forget to factor in closing costs (insurance, appraisals, attorney's fees, transfer taxes, loan fees, etc.) which normally range from 3% - 7% of the purchase price. Likewise, don't forget the following substantial continuing costs as well: monthly homeowner's insurance, property taxes (tax deductible), utilities, and maintenance.

• Get "pre-approved" (not just "pre-qualified") with a mortgage lender so you will know how much you can borrow and so you can move quickly if/when you find something you like.

• There are three tried and true methods of finding a place of your own: **drive around a neighborhood and look for "For Sale" signs** (not so easy in a tight housing market), **work with a real estate agent or broker** and **peruse the newspapers.** The Sunday *Boston Globe* and the Saturday edition of the *Boston Herald* are the primary source of real estate ads for the region; both papers have extensive real estate sections, with listing of condos and houses and their respective agencies.

• When looking at a home or a condo, if you have any question, no matter how 'dumb,' ask it; the better informed you are, the happier you'll be in the long run.

• Some real estate connoisseurs say that condos are better for social people (those who don't mind living in close proximity to others) and houses are better for the 'I want to be alone' types.

• Hire a professional safety inspector to check out a prospective home, even if it's a new one (they can have defects too). Go along on the safety inspection so you can discuss whatever is found. If you're in doubt about an appraisal or safety inspection, get a second opinion. It's usually worth it.

• When it comes time to make an offer, keep in mind that the simpler your offer is, the more likely the seller will understand it and accept it.

• The city of Boston offers a series of programs to make the buying process less intimidating and more manageable. The web site www.ci.ma.us/housing/homepurchase.html offers information on the ins and out of the mortgage and buying process, low-cost mortgages and grant programs that can help ease the process of buying a home.

• The Massachusetts Association of Realtors, 890-3700, and the Greater Boston Real Estate Board (GBREB), 423-8700, are two sources for names of real estate agents. Web sites for the Massachusetts Association of Realtors, (www.living.net) and the GBREB, (www.boardplace.com/gbreb) include a number of property listings, as well as advice on obtaining financing. The GBREB's site also offers software that can be downloaded to help prospective homeowners figure out how they can fit a mortgage into their budget. Also, most of the rental brokers listed above also handle residential sales. Finally, if you choose to work with a broker, remember that you don't have to go with the first one you find. Unless you absolutely can't wait, interview several and choose the person you feel most comfortable with.

• The Bank Rate Monitor internet site (www.bankrate.com) offers pages of information on mortages and interest rates at over 2000 banks. It pays to shop around.

• The needs assessment web site (www.te.com/filelist.htm) offers information on choosing a house, getting financing and insurance, conducting an inspection and saving on energy.

Other helpful web sites for would-be homeowners:

• **The National Association of Realtors** (www.realtor.com)
• **Homes and Land Magazine** (www.homes.com)
• **Fannie Mae** (www.fanniemae.com)
• **Realty Guide** (www.treb.com)
• **Home Scout** (www.homescout.com)
• **Abele Owner's Network** (www.owners.com)
• **Internet Real Estate Digest** (www.ired.com)

When moving from out of state you're caught in a catch-22 situation. You can't rent an apartment without a bank account and you can't get a bank account in your new city without an address. If you can find a place to live before you move out of your old home you'll be in a much better position. If you end up moving before you know precisely where you'll live, perhaps you shouldn't close out your old accounts before you have an address in Boston.

Once you've moved into your new Boston pad, your first order of business should be to open a bank account. Following is some information about money matters in the Boston area including checking and savings accounts, consumer complaint information, credit cards and various taxes.

BANKING

Most of the bigger banks in Boston have dozens of branches and hundreds of ATMs across the area, including Cape Cod. Smaller banks, too, will offer access to a wide network of ATMs, though they may charge you for this service.

Three of the largest consumer banks in the Boston area are:

- **BankBoston**, 800-226-7866 or 800-788-5000
- **Citizens**,800-922-9999
- **Fleet**, 800-225-5353

Shop around. Fees, products and quality of service vary.

A couple of things to keep in mind. First with all of the consolidation and mergers that are taking place in the financial services industry, if you want personal attention your best bet may be the one-branch "mom and pop" bank down the street from where you live. Second, if you belong to an organization (your employer, a union, a professional affiliation) that offers membership in a credit union, check it out. Credit unions offer some of the best bargains in banking.

CHECKING AND SAVINGS ACCOUNTS

It's easy to open checking or savings accounts — all you need is identification, an address and, of course, money. Once you've chosen your new bank you should probably open your new account at the branch closest to your home or work.

Today, some banks will even open a new account over the phone. They ask for your social security number, work information, income, etc. and then send you a confirmation package in the mail for you to sign and send back.

For fee-free checking, you'll need to maintain a certain monthly balance. Compare and save, as the saying goes.

You may want to open a savings account at the same time that you open your checking account though today interest rates on savings account balances are often so low as to be practically meaningless. Savings accounts should, however, be government insured which is important. Also, you may be allowed to connect your checking account with your savings account and use the combined monthly balance to calculate any account fees.

Other products and services to inquire about: debit cards, banking online or by-phone, statement vs. passbook savings, certificates of deposit, safe deposit boxes, hours, and, again, fees.

IN CASE OF CONSUMER COMPLAINT

The federal and state governments regulate bank policies on discrimination, credit, anti-redlining, truth-in-lending, etc. If you have a problem with your bank, your first step would be to attempt to obtain resolution directly from the bank. It this doesn't work or you're not satisfied with the results you can pursue the issue with the following agencies.

Nationally chartered commercial banks:

• **U.S. Comptroller of the Currency**, Consumer Division, Northeastern District - 114 Avenue of the Americas, Suite 3900, New York, NY 10036; 212-819-9860

Thrift institutions insured by the Savings Association Insurance Fund and/or federally chartered (i.e. members of the Federal Home

Loan Bank System):
• **U.S. Office of Thrift Supervision** - 745 Atlantic Avenue, Boston, MA 02111; 457-1900, (www.ots@treas.gov)

State chartered banks:

• **Massachusetts Division of Banks and Loans**, Consumer Assistance - 100 Cambridge Street, Boston 02202; 727-3145, (www.state.ma.us/dob)
• **Mortgage Review Board**, Massachusetts Division of Banks - 100 Cambridge Street, Boston 02202; 727-0529

State chartered banks that are members of the Federal Reserve System:

• **Federal Reserve Bank of Boston**, Bank Examination Division - 600 Atlantic Avenue, Boston 02106; 617-973-3000 ext. 3350, (www.bos.frb.org)
• **Federal Deposit Insurance Corporation** (FDIC), Compliance Division - 200 Lowder Brook Drive, Westwood, MA 02090; 781-320-1600

Federally chartered credit unions; state chartered credit unions with federal insurance:
• **National Credit Union Administration** - 9 Washington Square, Washington Avenue Extension, Albany, NY 12205; 518-464-4180

CREDIT CARDS

In case you've thrown away all those credit card offers that clutter up your mail box, you can call directly to request an application.

• American Express, 800-THE-CARD
• Diner's Club, 800-234-6377
• Discover Cards, issued through Morgan Stanley Dean Witter Financial, 800-347-2683.
• VISA and MasterCard can be obtained through banks and associations. Check your bank and shop around for the lowest interest rate.
• Department store credit cards are marketed at check-out counters. Often the store offers an incentive for you to fill out an application immediately — a discount off that day's purchases, etc. Any store

that offers store credit cards will send you an application form if you ever use a credit card for purchases at that store.

INCOME TAXES

Federal income tax forms can be obtained by calling 1-800-829-FORM. The public libraries and post offices are also sources for income tax forms. For taxpayer assistance call 1-800-829-1040. For recorded tax information call 800-829-4477 or 800-428-4732 (TTY).

The Internal Revenue Service branch in Boston is at the JFK Federal Building, Room E-100, Government Center, Boston, MA 02203.

Massachusetts resident tax forms can be obtained by calling 727-4392. You can also find them at Public Libraries, Post Offices and some banks. To find out which forms you'll need (especially if you haven't lived in Massachusetts for the whole tax year) call taxpayer assistance at 727-4545 or 800-392-6089.

The Massachusetts Department of Revenue's Boston office is located at 100 Cambridge Street, Boston 02202.

The Boston Bar Association has a Volunteer Income Tax Program that is generally held at the Boston Public Library's Copley Square branch. Call the Bar Association for exact dates, times and location: 617-742-0615.

OTHER TAXES

All Massachusetts residents who own a car that is registered in the Commonwealth of Massachusetts must pay an auto excise tax. The Registry of Motor Vehicles charges $25 per thousand dollar value of the blue book value of your vehicle. This excise tax is due thirty days from the date the notice is mailed. You are liable for this bill even if you never receive it so make sure you notify the Registry of any address changes. If you don't pay the tax, your car registration and driver's license can be suspended. For more information call the Registry of Motor Vehicles, 351-4500 or 800-858-3926.

Well, now you've successfully found your new home and set up your new bank account. This chapter will tell you how to get your utilities hooked up, your parking situation under control, and offer general information about how to get settled in Boston.

ELECTRICITY

Call **Boston Edison**, 262-9696, for electric service in **Arlington, Boston, Newton, Somerville, Watertown** and **Waltham.**

Normally landlords don't shut off the electricity at the end of the prior lease so you will usually just have to transfer the service into your name. Boston Edison customer service representatives will ask you standard questions over the phone and no deposit is required. If electric service wasn't extended throughout the vacancy, it should only take a day or two for Boston Edison to respond.

Massachusetts Electric, 888-211-1111, provides service to **Quincy** and **Medford.**

Call **Commonwealth Electric**, 800-642-7070, for electric service in **Cambridge.** Customer service personnel will process your application over the phone. You should call a week in advance, but they can usually respond within 24 hours.

If you are moving to **Belmont** you will have to fill out an application in person at the **Belmont Electric Light Department** located in Belmont Center at 450 Concord Avenue. You must show identification but no deposit is required. Service will be turned on in 24 hours. Call 484-2780 if you have questions.

$60.20 + tax
29th of month

TELEPHONE

In 1998, the number of area codes in Eastern Massachusetts was increased from two to four: 617, 508, 781, and 978. **Unless otherwise designated, the area code on a telephone number in this book is 617.**

In 1997, Bell Atlantic bought NYNEX and is now responsible for local telephone service in all of the areas listed in this book. You can call the following numbers to set up service anytime between 8:00 a.m. and 8:00 p.m., Monday through Friday. Saturday hours are 8:00 a.m. to 5:00 p.m. No deposit is required and it takes two to three days to be connected. There is a one time installation charge of $37.07 that can be spread out over four months. Customer service representatives will set up your long distance service with the long distance carrier of your choice when you call to set up local service.

Boston	
Charlestown	956-8000
Brookline	
Jamaica Plain	737-7530
Allston/Brighton	
Roslindale	
West Roxbury	329-8900
Cambridge	
Newton	
Waltham	
Watertown	873-1000
Arlington	
Belmont	
Somerville	662-3030

Bell Atlantic offers a variety of new services including call answering and caller ID. You can sign up for these and other services when you call to set up your local phone service.

Newburyport
$9.91
local package 54.95 + 3.45 wire serv.
plus
49.95
unlimited local
Call waiting · voice mail 24/7 no $5/mins · NJ
Boston, N. And.
free local + unlimited Eastern MA
stop telemarket
Boston, N. And.
override code # 3289 (pin #)

7/1 Tue. aft 1-5 pm

1 800 713 0000.

CELLULAR PHONES AND PAGING SERVICES

The Yellow Pages list numerous cellular phone and paging/beeper services. Here are a few to get you started.

#

978-463-3289

- **Cellular Phones**
  Cellular One, 800-235-5663
  Direct Cell, 800-439-2355
  New England Cellular, 800-481-1748
  Bell Atlantic Mobile Communications, 800-443-2355

  W/manages
  978
  462
  1118

- **Paging Services**
  Mobile Comm, 800-437-2337
  Metrocall, 800-542-6565
  Arch Paging, 800-443-4032 or 800-706-7243
  PageNet, 272-7243
  Air Touch Paging, 787-2337

start up PIN

GAS

Call **Boston Gas**, 742-8400, to set up gas service for your stove and hot water heater if you are moving to **Arlington, Belmont, Boston** (any section), **Medford, Newton, Quincy,** parts of **Somerville, Waltham. and Watertown.** Call in advance, especially during August and September when the students are moving. It could take ten days to get your gas service connected during that busy time period. Boston Gas can normally get you up and running within five days. Connection requires a home visit for which you must be present.

You can call Boston Gas from 8:00 a.m. to 5:00 p.m., Monday through Friday. They have no weekend hours and will not connect your service on Saturdays. You can request a morning or afternoon appointment but Boston Gas will not guarantee that you will see a representative during the time that you requested.

If you live in **Cambridge** or **other parts of Somerville**, call **Commonwealth Gas**, 800-572-9300, at least one day ahead of time. If the service has been turned off, someone must be at home to provide access to the meter as well as the apartment. They can't promise to be at your apartment at a specific time but they will promise you "between 8:00 a.m. and noon" or "between noon and 3:00 p.m." If you'd like, you can make an appointment for after 3:00 p.m. or on weekends for a $48 fee.

If you live in **Somerville** ask your landlord who supplies the gas — it could be either Commonwealth Gas or Boston Gas. Or, you can call either company and ask which company serves your address.

OIL

Oil is not supplied by a utility so you can choose your own oil supplier. Your landlord may already have a service agreement with an oil supplier to maintain the furnace burners and filters. However, if the choice is up to you, shop around. There are numerous oil suppliers listed in the Yellow Pages.

One option is to choose an oil cooperative. They generally charge you a membership fee of ten to fifteen dollars and your oil is then fifteen to twenty cents per gallon cheaper than normal rates from regular suppliers. The Boston area has two oil cooperatives:

- Boston Oil Consumers Alliance, 617-524-3950
- Ecological Innovations Oil Buying Network, 617-375-5882 or 800-649-7473

The following list of oil suppliers does not imply any endorsement. It is offered as a service to newcomers but you should, of course, shop around. Check the Yellow Pages as some suppliers only service certain areas or just the north shore or the south shore.

- Ashton Fuel, 623-0400
- Atlas Oil, 329-6800
- Benson Goss Fuels, 665-4047
- Bigelow Oil Co., 964-1600
- Brookline Oil Co., 734-0222
- Callendar Fuel, 436-7283
- Hughes, 327-4600
- Marvel Heat, 288-1800
- Metro Energy, 254-4856, 268-4662
- The Oil Express, 800-448-4328
- Star Five Oil Corp., 296-2509
- Supreme Fuel Co., 331-7900

IN CASE OF CONSUMER COMPLAINT
AGAINST UTILITIES AND OIL SUPPLIERS

The Massachusetts Department of Public Utilities (DPU) regulates companies that provide water, telephone, electric and gas services to retail
customers. The DPU's Consumer Division will respond to any questions
you have about billing, etc. Obviously you should try to resolve any dis-
putes you may have directly with the company in question. However, if
you are unsatisfied and/or wish to request a formal hearing, contact the
Consumer Division.

- **Massachusetts Department of Public Utilities**, Consumer Division,
  100 Cambridge Street, 12th Floor, Boston 02202; 617-727-3531.

- **The Massachusetts Department of Labor and Industries**, Division
  of Standards supervises the standards for household and auto fuels.
  If you have any questions or complaints about your oil distributor
  contact the Standards Division at 1 Ashburton Place, Room 1115,
  Boston 02108, 617-727-3480.

RECYCLING

Most cities and towns in the Boston area have some sort of recycling
program — curbside pickup of at least newspapers and/or drop-off centers for glass, plastic and metal.

BOSTON

Boston has residential curbside pick-up for one-to-six-family dwellings.
For people living in a larger building, check with the building superintendent. Pickup covers all recyclables, including newspaper and cardboard.
Plastic, glass, metals and beverage containers must be placed in a special
blue bin. To find out when pick-up is scheduled for your street and how
to get a blue box call Boston's **Recycling Hotline**: 617-635-4959.

The Yellow Pages includes a front section with other community
recycling information. Following is a partial list:

- **Allston/Brighton**
  Harvest Cooperative Supermarket parking lot, 449 Cambridge Street.

Hours: Monday through Saturday, 10:00 a.m. to 9:00 p.m.; Sundays, noon to 9:00 p.m.

- **Mission Hill**
  Boston Building Materials Coop, 100 Terrace Street, Roxbury
  Hours: all Saturdays, 9:00 a.m. to 3:00 p.m.

- **South End/Roxbury**
  Carter School at Northampton and Columbus (behind Mass. Ave. T Station)
  Hours: first Saturday of the month, 9:00 a.m. to 3:00 p.m.

- **Charlestown**
  Johnny's Foodmaster at the Bunker Hill Mall
  Hours: second Saturday of the month, 9:00 a.m. to 2:00 p.m.

- **East Boston**
  Harborside Community School, 312 Border Street
  Hours: second Saturday of the month, 9:00 a.m. to 2:00 p.m.

- **Dorchester**
  University of Massachusetts - Boston, Columbia Point Campus
  Hours: third Saturday of the month, 9:00 a.m. to 2:45 p.m.

- **Roslindale**
  Taft Hill Terrace parking lot (next to Kiddieland)
  Hours: fourth Saturday of the month, 9:00 a.m. to 3:00 p.m.

ARLINGTON

If you're moving into an apartment complex the manager or owner must call for a recycling box for you. If you're moving into a single-family dwelling, stop by the **Public Works Department** at 51 Grove Street to pick one up. In all other situations you can call 781-646-1000, ext. 5200, and request that a box be delivered. Also use this number to find out when your street is scheduled for pick-up.

BELMONT

If a recycling box has not been left behind by previous tenants, go to the **Highway Department** at 19 Moore Street (right across the street from the Light Department). You can call the Highway Department at 489-8210 for pick-up schedule information.

BROOKLINE

Curbside recycling is part of the town's refuse pick-up service. Brookline residents do pay for garbage pick-up; the cost is $41.50 per unit per year. If you move into a condo or single family dwelling, your garbage will automatically be picked up unless you specify otherwise. Most likely the cost of garbage pick-up has been factored into your rent when you move into an apartment, but you should check. To set up garbage pick-up or to request a recycling box call the **Public Works Department** at 730-2156.

CAMBRIDGE

Call the **Public Works Department** at 349-4800 to request a recycling box if the previous tenants didn't leave theirs behind or to find out the pick-up schedule.

MEDFORD

Curbside pickup is available for dwellings of one to four families. There is also a dropoff center at the **City Yard**, 21 James Street, 781-393-2402. Also call **Waste Management**, 781-933-2113, for more information.

NEWTON

Call the **Public Works Department** at 552-7200 to have a recycling box delivered and learn about the pick-up schedule.

QUINCY

To get a new recycling bin, you can go to the **Public Works Department**, 55 Sea Street, 770-2467, Monday-Friday 8:30-4:30 or Saturday 10-2.

SOMERVILLE

Drop by the **Department of Public Works** at 1 Franey Road to pick up a recycling box. You must have two proofs of residence (utility bill, lease, etc.). Call 635-0300 for office hours and scheduled pick-up times.

WALTHAM

Call the **Public Works Street Department** at 781-893-4040 for boxes and scheduled pick-up times.

WATERTOWN

You can drop off most recyclables, including yard waste and paper, at 195 Grove Street in East Watertown. Call **Watertown Recycling** at 972-6413 for details. Winter hours are: Monday, Wednesday and Thursday from 10:00 a.m. to 5:00 p.m. and 9:00 a.m. to 5:00 p.m. on Saturday and Sunday. Summer hours are: Monday, Wednesday and Thursday from noon to 7:00 p.m. and 9:00 a.m. to 5:00 p.m. on Saturday and Sunday.

DRIVER'S LICENSES, AUTOMOBILE REGISTRATION, PHOTO IDS

There are twelve **Registry of Motor Vehicle** branches in metro-Boston and two **Mall License Express** services where you can renew your license once you have it. Call 351-4500 for information. If this number is busy (and it usually is), try 351-9580.

The following registry branches are full service locations and are open between 8:45 a.m. and 5:00 p.m.:

• Lowell, 452 Chelmsford Street

- Malden, 180 Exchange Street
- Roslindale, 8 Cummings Highway

The following full service branches are also open on Thursday evenings until 7:00 p.m.:

- Main Office, 100 Nashua Street (closest T stop is North Station)
- Danvers, 95 Rosewood Drive
- Lawrence, 599 S. Union Street
- Quincy, 76 Ross Way
- Reading, 275 Salem (exit 40 off 128N)
- Watertown, 40 Spring Street

The Haverhill branch at 10 Welcome Street is open from 9:00 a.m. to noon and 1:00 p.m. to 4:00 p.m. on Monday and Friday.

The following Mall License Express locations are open Monday through Friday from 10:00 a.m. to 7:00 p.m. and Saturdays from 10:00 a.m. to 5:00 p.m.:

- Cambridgeside Galleria, 100 Cambridge Side Place
- Methuen Mall, 90 Pleasant Valley Street

Cash is not accepted at the Mall License Express locations.

To convert your out-of-state license to a Massachusetts state driver's license, submit a completed application with your old license at any of the branches listed above. You can either fill out the application when you get there or call and have one sent, 351-4500. New Hampshire drivers must also submit a copy of their driver's record. Conversion fees are $68.75 with an additional $15 for motorcycle designation.

To register your vehicle in Massachusetts, you must first insure your car in Massachusetts. Your insurance agent will fill out an application for registration and title form called RMV1. The agent must stamp and sign this form as well. Verify that all the information is correct before you sign it. This form, along with the out-of-state registration and/or title, must be taken to a Registry of Motor Vehicles. Usually the insurance agent will do this for you for a fee. The registration fee is $30 and the title fee is $50. If the car has been registered elsewhere for more than six months the car is exempt from Massachusetts state sales tax.

Massachusetts ID cards are available to Massachusetts residents of

18 years or older who do not have a driver's license. Bring three forms of identification to any of the registry branches listed above. Your birth certificate must be one of those pieces of identification. ID cards cost $15.

Massachusetts Liquor ID cards are available to Massachusetts residents who are 21 years of age or older who do not have a driver's license. They expire after five years and are issued only between 5:00 p.m. and 7:00 p.m. at registry offices that have evening hours, or at the main branch during the day.

If you are moving here from out of state you must provide three forms of identification: a birth certificate or passport, proof of address, and a cancelled check showing your signature. If you are a Massachusetts resident you must show your birth certificate, a high school year book with photo and a document with your signature. Liquor ID cards cost $15.

PARKING

Most cities suffer from too many cars trying to park in too few parking places. Boston's narrow, old streets make this common urban problem even worse because much of the city was built long before the invention of the automobile. This is especially true in the historic districts such as downtown, Back Bay, Beacon Hill, the North End and Charlestown. Parking spaces are limited during the spring, summer, and fall and are almost nonexistent in the winter when piles of snow cover many choice spots.

As the city of Boston's snow policy is one of reposition rather than removal after a heavy snowfall winter, parking wars are sure to break out in all Boston neighborhoods. Be advised: if you value your car's paint job or tires, think twice before removing a trash can, box or orange cone marking a shoveled parking space.

Now that you've been cowed into selling your car before moving to Boston you won't need the following information about parking permits and tickets.

PARKING PERMITS, PARKING TICKETS, TOWING

BOSTON

RESIDENT PARKING STICKERS

Many areas in Boston require cars to have resident stickers for legal on-street parking. The stickers are free, but the process to acquire one can be a hassle.

First you must insure and register your car in Boston. Your insurance agent can take care of registering it for you — usually for a small fee. But you must insure it in Boston first.

Once you've registered, bring your vehicle's registration documents and proof of residency to 224 Boston City Hall. Hours are Monday through Friday, 8:15 a.m. to 5:15 p.m. with extended hours on Thursday. Pay any parking tickets before you get there because you won't get a sticker if you have unpaid tickets. Proof of residence can be a utility bill, a bank statement, a mortgage statement, a credit card bill, or even a cable TV bill.

For more information call Resident Permits at the Office of the Parking Clerk (Transportation Department), 635-4682.

TICKETS AND TOWING
Boston's parking enforcement officials are so zealous that some Boston residents include a parking ticket fund in their monthly budgets. Tickets start at $10 to $20. If the ticket is unpaid after 21 days, the cost of the ticket rises to $16 to $25 dollars. If you have five overdue tickets your car may be booted and/or towed.

To find out if your car has been towed by the city for parking tickets or any other reason (such as a snow emergency) call **Public Information/Ticket Information at the Office of the Parking Clerk**, 635-4410.

To reclaim your towed car you must journey to either the second floor cashier area at Boston City Hall (hours are Monday through Friday, 9:00 a.m. to 5:30 p.m.) or to the Frontage Road tow lot (hours are Monday through Friday, 5:30 p.m. to 9:30 p.m. and Saturdays from 9:00 a.m. to noon). You must pay for the ticket(s), a seizure fee of $56, and storage fees which are $15/day or $3/hour up to a $15/day limit. You must pay with cash, money order, cashier's check or with MasterCard or Visa. The city does not accept personal checks.

Believe it or not, you can pay someone else to retrieve your towed car from the city lot, saving you the hassle of a trip downtown. **Freedom Ticket and Boot Removal Service**, 581-9275 will take care of your paperwork and set your wheels free for $25 plus 8% of whatever you owe.

COMMUTER PARKING
If you work in any of Boston's downtown areas and can't use public transportation, try to negotiate a parking space with your employer.

Some employers do offer parking spaces at garages and ramps for certain employees.

Ramp and garage prices cost $8 to $15 per day.

ARLINGTON

The Town of Arlington allows no overnight on-street parking. Therefore, you should make sure that your apartment or house includes a parking space or you could be in for an unpleasant surprise once you move in.

Visitor parking for overnight guests is allowed if you call the Arlington police and let them know. The police will need to know the license plate number of your guest's car.

Parking tickets in Arlington start at $10. If you have five or more tickets your car may be towed. The city uses five different towing companies so you should call the **Arlington Police** at 781-643-1212 to find out if your car was towed, where it was towed to and how to redeem it.

BELMONT

The town of Belmont also allows no overnight on-street parking for more than one hour between 1 a.m. and 7 a.m. If you have visitors, they can park overnight in one of several municipal lots in town. Belmont parking tickets start at $10 and you can call the **Parking Clerk** at 489-8252 if you have any questions.

If your car has been towed in Belmont, call the **Belmont Police** at 484-1215 to find out where it is and how to redeem it. You can also call the Police about overnight guest parking.

BROOKLINE

There is no overnight on-street parking in the town of Brookline, not even for visitors. You absolutely must make sure your Brookline apartment has off-street parking. Be prepared to pay $50-$100/month for a parking spot.

Tickets range from $10 to $100. Call the **Police Department's Traffic and Parking Clerk** at 730-2230 with questions. Brookline reserves the right to tow you after one unpaid parking ticket but more often they wait until you have five or more. There are other reasons for getting towed in Brookline, however, so check all signage carefully before parking!

CAMBRIDGE

There is little off-street parking in Cambridge and as in sections of Boston, you will need a **resident sticker** for your car to park on Cambridge streets. However, Cambridge stickers are not free.

Take $8, your registration (which shows that your car is registered in Cambridge) and proof of residence (a utility bill, etc.) to the **Parking Office of the Department of Traffic and Parking** at 57 Inman Street between 7:00 a.m. and 5:30 p.m. You can call 349-4700 with questions.

You can also obtain your resident sticker and guest passes at four of Cambridge's public libraries:

- North Cambridge Branch
- Central Square Branch
- Beaudreau/Observatory Branch
- East Cambridge Branch

The first three branches issue stickers between 1:00 p.m. and 8:00 p.m., Monday through Friday. The East Cambridge branch issues stickers between 1:00 p.m. and 5:00 p.m. Monday through Friday.

Cambridge tickets range between $5 and $50. For **parking ticket information** call 349-4705. To find out **if your vehicle has been towed** call 349-3306.

Sometimes the police will have no towing record of your car. Before your heart fails at the thought that your car may be stolen, look around the area where you parked. If you parked illegally in a parking lot, often the phone number of the tow company that services that parking lot will be posted. You should also ask at a neighboring restaurant or gas station about who the likely towing company may be.

Cambridge has a number of ordinances that make the winter parking wars more bearable than in Boston. First: it is illegal to mark a parking space with anything. Police remove items left in the street and ticket the owners if possible. Second: the city of Cambridge recently passed an ordinance requiring car owners to shovel out their cars within 72 hours of a snow storm. It frees up a lot of space if you don't have snow covered hunks of metal hibernating on your street.

MEDFORD

Overnight on-street parking in Medford is allowed on either the odd or even side of the street in winter. If the current year ends in an even number, then parking is allowed on the even side of the street. If the year ends in an odd number, then you can park on the odd side. In November 1998, parking will be allowed on the even side of the street from midnight to 7 a.m. The city's main streets are designated snow emergency routes, thus no parking is allowed during snowstorms. Tickets range from $5 to $50. For more information call the **Parking Clerk** at 781-393-2440.

NEWTON

Overnight on-street parking restrictions in the City of Newton are seasonal. There is no overnight parking on the streets from November 1 through April 30.

Tickets range from $5 to $50. Call the **Parking Office** for information: 552-7087. You can be towed after five or more overdue, unpaid tickets. Call the **Newton Police** at 552-7240 to find out whether or not you've been towed.

QUINCY

Quincy has two large parking areas, the city-owned parking garage on Ross Way and a city-owned Hancock lot near City Hall. An **overnight parking permit** is required for parking from midnight to 8 a.m. Parking is limited to two or four hours near T stations, depending on the neighborhood. Tickets range from $5 to $50. Call the **Parking Clerk** at 376-1060 for more information.

SOMERVILLE

Somerville requires **resident stickers** for on-street parking. Take your registration (which shows that your car is registered in Somerville) and $1 to the **Traffic and Parking Department** at 133 Holland Street, 625-6600 ext. 7900. For guest passes all you need to show is a utility bill.

Somerville allows you five unpaid, overdue tickets before you are booted and/or towed. If your car has been towed in Somerville, call **Pat's Towing Service** directly at 354-4000.

WALTHAM

Overnight on-street parking is not allowed in the City of Waltham, unless posted signs say otherwise. Parking ticket questions may be asked at the **Treasurer's Office**: call 781-893-4040.

Waltham doesn't bother with towing your car. Instead, the registry marks your license after three unpaid, overdue tickets. With a mark against your license you are unable to renew your driver's license or car registration. Tickets range from $12 to $50.

WATERTOWN

Overnight on-street parking is not allowed in the Town of Watertown either. Tickets are sent to City Hall and you can call the **Town Clerk** with questions at 617-972-6486.

Tickets range from $10 to $100 and it can take 15 tickets before your car will be towed in Watertown. Call the **Traffic Division of the Watertown Police** for information about a towed car at 972-6549 or about guest parking.

STOLEN CARS

When you move to the Boston area it is recommended that you consider your car's security and photocopy your title, registration and proof of insurance.

Many car owners in Boston invest in some sort of antitheft device. These range from simple steering wheel locks to electronic alarms to systems that shut off your engine if a secret code isn't punched in after the engine has been started. Yes, they are expensive but so is buying a new car.

If your car is missing, first make sure you know which town you parked in (boundaries can get blurry for newcomers) before you call to find out if it has been towed. Once you're sure it hasn't been towed you must go to the police precinct that has jurisdiction over the area from which the car was stolen and fill out a report (see the Neighborhood sections for precinct addresses and phone numbers). You will need your vehicle ID number, the title if you have it, and the license plate number. If you have photocopied your title, registration and proof of insurance your task will be much easier.

Also, it is a good idea to store a copy of your title, etc., because when the police recover a stolen vehicle, the registration and proof of insurance are not always in the car anymore. Dealing with replacing those items adds insult to injury — and costs money as well. Having photocopies of those documents makes the process a little easier.

VOTER REGISTRATION

Massachusetts law requires you to register to vote in person, but you can go to any city or town hall in the state and register to vote in your city or town. Therefore, you can register wherever is most convenient for you. You will need proof of residence which can be a lease, a utility bill or a driver's license.

You may only vote in a primary election if you are enrolled in a party. If you enroll in a political party it does not affect your right to vote in the general election.

If you choose to remain an "independent," check the box beside "no party or designation" or "unenrolled" on the registration form. As an independent you may choose any party ballot you wish at the state and presidential primaries. However, once you choose a party ballot you become automatically enrolled in that political party. If you want to return to independent status you must fill out a card as you leave the voting area.

Following is a listing of voter registration sites at city and town halls for the areas listed in this guide:

BOSTON

Go to the Election Department at **Boston City Hall, room 241** between 9:00 a.m. and 5:00 p.m., Monday through Friday. Boston City Hall is located at Government Center and is easily reached by public transportation. When election days approach, the Elections Department opens other places around the city where you can register. Call 635-4635 for places and hours of operation.

ARLINGTON

The Town Hall is located at 730 Massachusetts Ave. Go to the Town Clerk's office on the second floor any time between 9:00 a.m. and 5:00 p.m., Monday through Friday. Call 781-646-1000 ext. 4056 with questions.

BELMONT

Go to the Town Clerk's Office at the Town Hall Building at 455 Concord Avenue, 489-8201. The office is open from 8:00 a.m. to 8:00 p.m. on Mondays and 8:00 a.m. to 4:00 p.m., Tuesday through Friday.

BROOKLINE

The Town Hall is located at 333 Washington Street. Go to the Town Clerk's Office, 730-2010, from 8:00 a.m. to 5:00 p.m., Monday through Thursday and 8:00 a.m. to 12:30 p.m. on Friday.

CAMBRIDGE

Cambridge's Election Commission is located on the third floor of the Police Station at Central Square, 349-4361. As in Boston, Cambridge's Elections Commission opens up additional voter registration spots as election days approach. Call the Commission for details.

MEDFORD

Medford's Election Commission at City Hall, 85 George P. Hassett Drive, 781-393-2490, is open 8:30 a.m. to 5:00 p.m., Monday through Friday.

NEWTON

Go to the Elections Commission Department at City Hall, 1000 Commonwealth Avenue, between 8:30 a.m. and 5:00 p.m., Monday through Friday. The phone number is 552-7041.

QUINCY

Quincy's Election Commission is located at City Hall, 1305 Hancock Street, 376-1142. The Commission is open 8:30 a.m. to 5:00 p.m., Monday through Friday.

SOMERVILLE

The Election Department is found at Somerville City Hall, 93 Highland Avenue (corner of Highland and School). The Department is open Monday through Friday from 8:30 a.m. to 4:30 p.m.. Call 625-6000 ext. 4200 with questions.

WALTHAM

The City Clerk's office is located in the City Hall, 610 Main Street, 781-893-4040 ext. 3056. Hours are Monday, Wednesday and Friday from 8:30 a.m. to 4:30 p.m. and Tuesday and Thursday from 8:30 a.m. to 1:00 p.m..

WATERTOWN

The Town Clerk's office is at the Town Hall, 149 Main Street (next to the library), 972-6488. It is open from 8:30 a.m. to 5:00 p.m., Monday through Friday.

LIBRARY CARDS

Boston's main library at Copley Square was the first large city library ever opened for the general public in the United States. With the exception of Somerville, most of the Boston area libraries are networked so if you have a library card in one city or town you will be able to check out books from libraries in many others. Library locations are listed in the neighborhood profiles. Check your neighborhood profile for the library closest to you. The following section lists the identification requirements for the library systems mentioned in this book:

The **Boston** library system requires proof of Massachusetts residence and some sort of ID with your signature on it (it doesn't have to be a photo ID).

Arlington, Brookline, Belmont, Medford, Newton, Quincy, Somerville, Waltham and Watertown libraries need proof of your residence in that town. If your license doesn't show your current address you can use your checkbook (if it has your current address imprinted), a piece of mail with your address on it or your lease.

The **Cambridge** library system requires two forms of identification, one with your photograph on it (a passport or driver's license) and one with your address (your lease or a piece of mail).

You may be able to use many of the college and university library systems however in most cases you will not be allowed to check out materials.

PASSPORTS

You can apply for a passport at the **Tip O'Neill Federal Building,** 10 Causeway, Room 247, Monday through Friday from 9:00 a.m. to 4:00 p.m.. The nearest T stop is North Station. Call 565-6990 for recorded information on the process. Processing time usually takes three weeks but can take longer depending on when you apply. If you have an after hours, life or death emergency you can call 202-647-4000.

TELEVISION STATIONS

Boston television viewers can pick up broadcasts from New Hampshire and Rhode Island as well as Boston so you'll find a lot of network repetition as you channel surf.

Channel 2, WGBH-TV, PBS
Channel 4 , WBZ-TV, CBS
Channel 5 , WCVB-TV, ABC
Channel 6 , WLNE-TV, CBS

Channel 7 , WHDH-TV, NBC
Channel 9 , WMUR-TV, ABC
Channel 10 , WJAR-TV, NBC
Channel 11 , WENH-TV, PBS
Channel 12 , WPRI-TV, ABC
Channel 25 , WFXT-TV, FOX
Channel 27 , WUNI-TV, independent (Worcester)
Channel 38 , WSBK-TV, UPN
Channel 44 , WGBX-TV, PBS
Channel 50 , WNDS-TV, independent (Derry, NH)
Channel 56 , WLVI-TV, independent
Channel 60 , WGOT-TV, independent (Merrimack, NH)
Channel 62 , WMSP-TV, independent
Channel 68 , WABU-TV, independent

CABLE TELEVISION

If you must have your MTV, consult the following list for the cable carrier in your town or city. (Each town has only one carrier):

- Cablevision of Boston (all sections), 787-6616
- Cablevision of Brookline, 731-0373
- Media One of Cambridge/Arlington, 888-633-4266 or 876-3939
- Media One of Newton, 449-6960
- Media One of Watertown, 923-4300
- Media One of Waltham, 781-893-6447
- Cablevision of Nashoba, 271-0103, serves Belmont
- Time-Warner Cable, 397-8600, serves Somerville

Cable television is regulated by both the commonwealth and your municipality.

Massachusetts Cable Television Antenna Television Commission, 100 Cambridge St., Room 2003, Boston 02202, 727-6925
Boston Office of Cable Communications, 43 Hawkins Street, Boston 02114, 635-3112 ext.460

SAFETY

Like all large American cities, Boston has its share of crime. Fortunately, the crime rates in most major American cities have seen a decrease in the past decade. That said, there are a few common sense things that a newcomer to Beantown should keep in mind:

- Trust your intuition. If something doesn't feel right, go with it. You're not being paranoid, you're feeling healthy survival instincts.
- When outside, keep your eyes and ears open. Always remaining alert and aware of your surroundings is key to personal crime prevention.
- Never let a stranger get in your car, and don't get in a car with a stranger. Studies show that once you are in a vehicle with a would-be criminal, your chances of survival decrease dramatically.
- Don't move into a neighborhood where you don't feel comfortable. Before you take an apartment, walk around the neighborhood at different times of the day to give yourself an impression of what the area is like.
- Protect your apartment or home from potential intruders. For example, in a ground floor or garden apartment, you should probably have sturdy bars on your windows. Check your door for a deadbolt. If it doesn't have one, request that your landlord install one for you. Always err on the side of caution when assessing your risk.
- On public transportation, try and sit in a car or area with other people.
- Resist the temptation to travel alone or at night through a neighborhood of which you are afraid or uncertain.
- If you find yourself in a situation where your life may be in danger, run, scream, fight, whatever it takes to save your life. In such a situation, being passive may not be the best response.
- A useful guide for those on the go is *Smart Business Travel: How to Stay Safe When You're on the Road* by Stacey Abarbanel.
- Report crime. No matter what, when you see a crime take place, call 911. Your concern may help someone else in need. For non-emergency police questions, call 343-4200; they can tell you the location of your nearest District or Area police headquarters.

I f you've arrived in Boston without any feathers for your nest, have no fear —you can rent them all. Additionally, Boston offers some of the best service-providers anywhere. In this chapter, we'll start off with the basics including daycare and babysitting.

DAYCARE AND BABYSITTING

Boston has many two-income families with small children so locating quality childcare here can be a competitive and expensive proposition. If you're pregnant, looking for daycare should be part of your pre-natal activities because it can take a year or more to get your child into your chosen daycare facility. Salting away money for regular child care should also be a prenatal activity: daycare in the Boston area can easily run over $1,000 a month.

The Boston Parent's Paper, a free publication, has many listings and advertisements that may prove invaluable to you in your search. Don't forget the **Yellow Pages**. Check under "Child Care Centers" and "Nanny Service and Sitting Services."

The **Child Care Resource Center**, 130 Bishop Allen Drive, Cambridge 02139, 547-9861, provides information and referral on day-care programs. The Center serves Cambridge, Arlington, Belmont, Brookline, Newton, Somerville, and Watertown but NOT Boston. The City of **Cambridge** also has a **Child Care Division** in its Human Services Department. Call 349-6200 for details.

If you're a total stranger with no family or friends in the area who can help during the transition period, you might consider hiring a nanny temporarily while you find the right situation for your child. Depending on the age of your child, a nanny might also be the best long-term solution if you can afford it. Most pre-schools do not accept children unless they are potty trained and it's hard to potty train your child if s/he is in daycare. Although inclusion in this guide is not an endorsement, here are some possibilities for nanny hunting:

- **Boston Nanny Centre, Inc.,** 527-0114
- **Child Care Placement Services,** 566-6294
- **Minute Women, Inc.,** 227-1889 or 862-3300
- **Nannies Nook, Inc.,** 749-8097
- **The Nanny Connection,** 749-8549

Keep in mind that you don't have to use a Boston agency to get a Boston nanny. Therefore, you may want to try a local agency *before* you move here. Additionally, many nannies from all over the country are willing to travel to the East Coast for employment so using a national agency may also be an option for you.

If you don't want or can't afford a nanny and you move to Boston in the summer you should be able to find a high school or college student experienced in child care. The summer might just be long enough for you to make arrangements for permanent or long-term care. If your children are older, requiring a watchful eye only between the time they get home from school and the time you get home from work, consider hiring one of the hundred thousand college students in the area.

If you are interested in signing up for daycare services, be aware that preregistration is required at all providers.

In addition, a Notice of Medical History from the child's doctor must accompany your application. Two services to be aware of: occasional daycare and daycare for sick children. Of course, not all providers offer these options, but some do, and if you're interested in them, you should ask.

Bright Horizon, 39 Brighton Avenue in Allston (formerly Hamilton's Children's Center), 789-4323, is one of the daycare services that will take care of your healthy child when your normal arrangements fall through. Occasional care costs $8 per hour; five days a week will run you a hefty $1,214 per month.

RENTAL SERVICES

If you streamlined your existence to make your move more aerodynamic, you can stay unencumbered by renting what you need rather than purchasing. A word of caution though: read the rental agreement before you sign it, and don't agree to anything you don't understand.

FURNITURE

Most offer same-day delivery and short-term, long-term or "rent-to-own" agreements. Bring a drawing of your floor plan with measurements. Here are some places to consider (inclusion in this guide is not an endorsement):

- **Cort Furniture Rental**, 155 North Beacon Street, Brighton, 254-5455; 98 Boylston, Boston, 542-8383
- **Putnam Furniture Leasing Co.**, 354-1506, 614 Mass. Ave., Cambridge; 929 Worcester Road, Framingham, 508-879-8383
- **Rainbow Rentals**, 375 Main Street, Malden, 781-397-8300; 942 Hyde Park Ave., Hyde Park, 361-1900
- **Universal Furniture Rentals, Inc.**, 540 Atlantic Avenue, Boston, 800-966-7115; 1590 Concord Street, Framingham, 508-788-0700

TELEVISION AND VCR

More than likely you would be able to rent a TV and/or VCR from the same place that you rented your furniture. However, there are some places that specialize in electronic equipment.

- **Bill's TV Rental**, 77 Winn Street, Woburn, 781-933-8866
- **Colortyme TV Rental**, 541 Columbia Road, Dorchester, 288-2265; 15-17 Corinth, Roslindale, 469-3503
- **Prudential TV**, 1639 Washington Street, Boston, 267-5544; Brookline andWest Roxbury 536-6722; Somerville and Cambridge 266-2224
- **Rainbow Rentals**, see listing in **Furniture** above
- **Rent-A-Center** has twelve locations in the Boston area. Check the Yellow Pages for phone numbers and addresses.

PERSONAL COMPUTERS

Most PC rental businesses offer same-day delivery and set-up and maintenance agreements.

- **Fox Computer Rentals**, Boston, 628-8500; Framingham, 508-872-6223

- **GE Rental/Lease,** Woburn, 781-935-2280
- **PCR Personal Computer Rentals,** 194 Forbes Road, Braintree, 781-356-5700; 57 Commerce Way, Woburn, 781-933-5993; Boston, 695-9991
- **Rentex Computer Rentals,** Boston, 423-5567
- **Schneider Leasing Company,** 451 D Street, South Boston, 261-6060
- **The Rental Network,** 240 Bear Hill Road, Waltham, 781-890-7088

HOUSE CLEANING SERVICES

In addition to regular house cleaning, most services also offer special one day cleaning arrangements for moving days (either in or out) or for fire restoration.

- **Chapman Home Cleaning Service, Inc.,** 512 Park Drive, Boston, 266-6622
- **Maid in the USA,** Boston, 482-3500
- **Maid Pro,** 25 Myrtle Street, Boston, 742-8080
- **McMaid,** 238 Broadway, Cambridge, 354-7788
- **Merry Maids** has nine offices. Check the Yellow Pages for the branch that serves your area.

MAIL RECEIVING SERVICES

If you're in between addresses but need a place to receive mail, you can rent a box at the post office. If your life doesn't fit into the postal service's schedule you may want to try a private service. Mail Boxes Etc. typically has slightly longer hours than the post office. However, for middle of the night emergencies, there is a 24-hour post office at South Station, 25 Dorchester Avenue. Many of the following services will also forward your mail to you — even overseas if necessary.

- **Bette James & Associates,** 678 Mass. Ave., Cambridge, 661-2622
- **Delta Letter Drop,** 310 Franklin Street, Boston, 423-3543
- **Mail Boxes Etc.** has thirteen branches in the Boston area. Check the Yellow Pages for details.

MOVING AND STORAGE

There are pages and pages of movers and moving services listed in the

Yellow Pages. Moving is stressful under ideal circumstances and miserable when you're having a problem with your moving company. After all, you're entrusting all of your possessions to strangers. Make sure you know what your rights are.

The **Commercial Motor Vehicles Division, Division of Transportation,** Mass. Dept. of Public Utilities, 100 Cambridge Street, Room 1203, Boston, 727-3559, regulates transportation of property within Massachusetts and licenses intrastate carriage. This Division regulates price rates of household and business movers and has full police powers to enforce all regulations. Division staff will advise consumers on the proper procedure to rectify overcharges and will accept complaints about pick-up, deliver, damages, etc. This division does not regulate self-moving truck lines such as U-Haul, Ryder, etc.

Interstate moving and delivery companies are regulated by the **Interstate Commerce Commission**, 99 Summer Street, Fifth Floor, Boston, MA 02110, 424-5760. Ask for the duty officer for complaint forms.

You may have to store some or all of your furniture depending on whether you have an apartment and the size of that apartment. There are also pages and pages of storage warehouses in the Yellow Pages. The **Licensing Section, Massachusetts Dept. of Public Safety**, 1 Ashburton Place, Room 1310, Boston, 727-3692 licenses and accepts written complaints about public warehouses.

CONSUMER PROTECTION

There are a number of private organizations in Massachusetts that provide information about businesses and consumer issues. Some will assist you in resolving your complaints. It's always a good idea to check up on any service before you enter into an agreement. This is a place to start.

- **Council of Better Business Bureaus (CBBB)** - 20 Park Plaza, Suite 820, Boston, 426-9000. Publishes free brochures. Offers general information of products and services. Offers reliability reports and background information on local businesses and organizations.
- **MassPIRG (Massachusetts Public Interest Research Group)** - 29 Temple Place, Boston, 292-4800. A nonprofit advocacy and research organization committed to protecting consumers and the environment. Provides information and referral on a variety of consumer and environmental issues. Reports on a wide variety of topics are available for $5 each.

- **Massachusetts Bar Association, Tel-Law** - 20 West Street, Boston, 542-9069. 24-hour information tape on legal issues.
- **WBZ Call for Action** - 1170 Soldiers Field Road, Allston, 787-7070. Telephone information and referral on problems handled by agencies or institutions.

FEDERAL AND STATE AGENCIES ARE AS FOLLOWS:

- **Massachusetts Executive Office of Consumer Affairs and Business Regulation** - 1 Ashburton Place, 4th Floor, Room 1411, Boston, 727-7780
- **Division of Registration Investigation Unit**, 100 Cambridge Street, 15th Floor,Boston; 727-7406
- **Consumer Protection Division, Mass. Dept. of the Attorney General** - 131 Tremont Street, 1st Floor, Boston; 727-8400
- **Mass. Board of Bar Overseers** - 75 Federal Street, Boston; 357-1860
- **Federal Trade Commission** - 101 Merrimac Street, Suite 801, Boston, 424-5960
- **Consumer Product Safety Commission** - 10 Causeway Street, Room 469, Boston, 565-7730

SERVICES FOR THE HANDICAPPED/DISABLED

Boston has made great strides to serve the needs of disabled residents and visitors, especially with the passage of the federal Americans with Disabilities Act in 1990. Just about every curb has been rebuilt for easy wheelchair accessibility, and most public buildings have special entrances to make it easier for the disabled. There is a well-coordinated effort within the public and private sector to ensure that the disabled are not forgotten. Here are some of the services, organizations and resources that help make it easier for a new Bostonian to live safely and conveniently.

GETTING AROUND

- **The Ride** - An individual ride program operated by the **MBTA** and offered to allMassachusetts residents who can't use regular trains, subways or buses. It's $3 for a disabled pass and 50 cents for a senior pass, and then an additional charge of 20 cents on the rails and 15 cents on the bus. Passes of up to a month are also available to visitors. For more information contact The Ride, 10 Park

Plaza,Room 4730, Boston 02116, 222-5123, 800-533-6282, TTY 222-5415.

- **Bus Service** - Bus lines with wheelchair access are marked on maps and schedules. There are about 50 routes that are 100 percent handicapped accessible, and about 80 percent on other routes. But even if a route isn't fully accessible, calling ahead to 800-Lift-Bus guarantees that the driver will be aware of a special needs case. Customer service/travel information 222-3200, TTY 222-5146.
- **Subways and Commuter Rails** - About half of the MBTA's subway and commuter rail stations are handicap accessible with elevators and car-level platforms. The latest elevator conditions in all MBTA accessible stations is available through the **MBTA Elevator Update line** at 222-2828. The T's web site is www.mbta.com.
- **Transportation Access Pass** - The application must be filled out by a licensed healthcare professional. Call 222-5976 for an application.
- **The MBTA's Senior Pass Program and Access Pass Program** - Available to persons 65 years or older. Applications available at MBTA Back Bay Station, 145 Dartmouth Street, Boston 02116-5162, or call 222-5438, TTY 222-5854.
- **Handicapped License Plates and Parking Permits for People with Disabilities** - An application, available through the Medical Affairs Branch of the Registry of Motor Vehicles, has to be filled out by a certified physician before it's submitted for approval. P.O. Box 199100, Roxbury 02119. Call 351-9222. Web site is www.mag-net.state.ma.us/rmv.
- **Taxis** - Many Boston taxi companies have accessible cabs. **Veterans Taxi** specializes in accessible transportation. 527-0300.

COMMUNICATION

Bell Atlantic offers a range of special equipment for people in Massachusetts who are blind, deaf, hard of hearing, vision or speech impaired and mobility impaired. The special equipment and services include amplified phones, big-button or memory-button phones, TTY, and cordless and speaker phones. You must be a Massachusetts resident to qualify for free telephone equipment.

The Bell Atlantic **Customer Contact Center for Individuals with Disabilities** is at 251 Locke Drive, Marlboro, 01752, 800-974-6006 (voice and TTY).

Massachusetts Relay is an operator service that connects TTY with voice service and vice versa. Voice service is 800-439-0183. TTY service is 800-439-2370.

OTHER RESOURCES

Massachusetts provides a variety of public and private services for handicapped or disabled newcomers. Following is a list of governmental and private agencies:

- **Association of Late Deafened Adults**, P.O. Box 611, Newton, 02160, 923-2447 TTY. E-mail address: CAMenton@aol.com
- **Bay State Council of the Blind**, 57 Grandview Avenue, Watertown, 02172, 923-4519.
- **Boston Center for Independent Living**, 95 Berkeley Street, Suite 206, Boston, 02116, 338-6666 (voice), 338-6662 (TTY).
- **Braille and Talking Book Library at the Perkins School for the Blind**, 175 North Beacon Street, Watertown, 924-3434.
- **Commission for Persons with Disabilities**, 635-3682.
- **Guide Dog Users of Massachusetts**, 566-4478.
- **Massachusetts Office on Disability** provides details of the law and rights. The MOD is located at One Ashburton Place, Room 1305, Boston, 02108, 727-7440 or 800-322-2020 outside of Boston.
- **Massachusetts Network Information Provider for People with Disabilities**, 642-0248 or 800-642-0249.
- **Massachusetts Law Reform Institute**, 99 Chauncy Street, Boston, 357-0700.
- **Massachusetts Rehabilitation Commission** provides vocational rehabilitation. Fort Point Place, 27-43 Wormwood Street, Boston, 02210, 204-3600 (voice).
- **Massachusetts Commission for the Deaf and Hard of Hearing** handles requests for interpreters and Computer Aided Real Time Translation (CART) reporters. 210 South Street, Boston 02111, 695-7500 or 800-249-9949 (voiceand TTY).
- **Massachusetts Commission for the Blind**, 88 Kingston Street, Boston, 02111, 727-5550.
- **Massachusetts Assistive Technology Partnership** provides information about devices that make it easier to live and get around, such as stairlifts, big-button telephones, BrailleMate, vibrating alarm clocks, bed shakers, bottle openers, voice synthesizers, and voice-activated computer phone amplifiers. Children's Hospital, 1295 Boylston Street, Suite 310, Boston, 02215, 800-848-8867

voice/TTY, www.matp.org.
- **Massachusetts Network of Information Providers** has general disability-related information. 800-642-0249 or 781-642-0248.
- **Museums** — Museums in the Boston area have an access coordinator for the disabled. At the **Museum of Fine Arts** contact 267-9300, ext. 302. At the **Museum of Science** contact 589-0419.
- **New England ADA Technical Assistance Center** provides information related to the Americans with Disabilities Act. 374 Congress Street, Suite 301, Boston, 02110, 800-949-4232 (voice/TTY).
- **Very Special Arts** is a non-profit organization that helps make it possible for people with disabilities to participate in Boston's arts and culture scene, 350-7713, www.vsamass.org.

PET SERVICES

Owning pets in a big city makes you a member of a special fraternity, one with many responsibilites. Not only is it necessary to clean up after your dog on walks, there is also the care for cats, birds and more exotic animals to consider. Going for a simple stroll with your pooch is a great way to strike up conversations and meet new people. As a newcomer, your animal companion can help break the ice between and your new neighbors.

Boston boasts one of the country's top animal hospitals, **Angell Memorial Animal Hospital**, 350 South Huntington Avenue, Jamaica Plain, 522-7282, which provides 24-hour emergency services and can be used as a referral for veterinary services as well as provide such special care as oncology treatment and X-rays. In other words, a person seeking treatment for a pet iguana, turtle or parrot can turn to Angell Memorial.

The **Boston Cat Hospital** in Kenmore Square, 665 Beacon Street, 266-7877, specializes in felines.

Generally the best source for information on veterinarians is via word of mouth, so talk with new neighbors, go for a walk in the park, or call the **Massachusetts Society for the Prevention of Cruelty to Animals**, 350 South Huntington, 522-5055, where information is also available about adopting a new pet.

The **Animal Rescue League of Boston**, 10 Chandler Street, 426-9170, has an adoption center open daily, and you can call the **Alliance for Animals**, for information on affordably spaying a pet, 232 Silver Street, South Boston, 268-7800.

It is a state law that dogs be licensed. Contact the **Animal Control Office at Boston City Hall**, Room 811, 635-5348, and be sure to let them know if the animal has been spayed or neutered, since the fee for unfixed dogs is lower ($17 vs. $6). Another suggestion; let a new vet know you want any dog that is two years or older to receive a three-year rabies shot instead of a one-year shot.

Dogs need to be walked two or three times a day, and there are a number of credible services that will provide this for fees ranging from $10 per walk during the week and $12.50 on weekends, to home sitting for all pets at up to $45 a day.

Besides normal medical care for pets, there are even services in the area for people wishing to get their pets into show business, including **Animal Actors** in Weymouth and **Animal Episodes** in Ipswich. On the other end of the spectrum, several groups are devoted to the fight against animal exploitation, including **Citizens to End Animal Suffering & Exploitation**, the **Massachusetts Society for the Prevention of Cruelty to Animals** and the **World Society for the Protection of Animals.**

Boston's shopping scene certainly offers variety. If you're the kind of person who knows exactly what you want and you don't want to waste any time getting it — no problem. You can get anything you want once you know where to look. And if your idea of a wild week-end is one spent in pursuit of the most unusual boutique you can find, Boston will keep you busy for a long time.

You can spend as much or as little as you want. You can join a coop-erative or just shop at one. Stores of the same variety tend to cluster together in the same area. So, for example, if you hear about a great sport-ing goods store on **Commonwealth Avenue** make sure you check around once you get there because you're likely to find two or three others.

The downtown area has a number of shopping districts. Try **Downtown Crossing** and **Washington Street**. Check out **Charles Street** and **Cambridge Street** on Beacon Hill. Don't forget **Faneuil Hall, Quincy Market, the Haymarket area, and Chinatown**.

Back Bay shopping clusters around **Boylston and Newbury Streets**. Also check out **Copley Place** and the **Shops at the Prudential Center**, connected by a covered pedestrian bridge. Downtown and Back Bay tend to close early so call ahead to make sure that boutique or gallery is open before you endure both traffic and parking hassles to get there.

In Cambridge, take a drive or a walk along **Massachusetts Avenue** and stop at any of the squares. Try **Broadway** and **Middlesex Avenue** in Somerville. Watertown's **Arsenal Mall** inhabits an old U.S. government arsenal. Take a drive or a walk along **Harvard Street** in Brookline and Allston/Brighton. Don't forget **Commonwealth Avenue, Beacon Street** and **Washington Street**. **Route 9** and **Route 1** feature a more suburban, mall or strip mall set-up.

If you have a lot to do and want to get it over with in one fell swoop, consider a full-service department store. If shopping is a form of recreation or sport for you, take the time to get to know metro Boston. You may want to spend an afternoon on **Newbury Street** searching for the perfect plant stand or lithograph.

DEPARTMENT STORES

- **Bloomingdale's**, Chestnut Hill Mall on Route 9, Newton, 630-6000
- **B.U. Bookstore Mall**, 660 Beacon (Kenmore Square), Boston 267-8484. Not just a bookstore, this six-level Kenmore Square shopping mall offers clothing, appliances, word processors, phones, prints, etc.
- **Harvard/MIT Cooperative Society,** known as the "Coop" and pronounced like "chicken coop." The two main locations are at Harvard Square, 1400 Mass. Ave., 499-2000 and Kendall Square, 3 Cambridge, 499-3200. The Coop is a cooperative that Harvard, MIT, Wheelock and the Massachusetts College of Pharmacy students, faculty, alumni and employees can join. Members earn a rebate annually that is based on what they've spent throughout the year. The Coop sells everything from appliances to deodorant.
- **Macy's**, 450 Washington Street, Boston, 357-3000 and 181 Middlesex Avenue, Somerville, 666-4000
- **Lord & Taylor,** 760 Boylston Street, Boston, 262-6000 and 39 Dalton Street, Boston, 262-6009
- **Neiman-Marcus**, 5 Copley Place, Boston, 536-3660
- **Saks Fifth Avenue**, Prudential Plaza, Boston, 262-8500

DISCOUNT DEPARTMENT STORES

- **Ann & Hope,** 615 Arsenal Street, Watertown, 924-3400
- **Bradlees,** 550 Arsenal Street, Watertown, 926-4410; 180 Somerville Ave., Somerville, 628-3426; 950 American Legion Parkway, Roslindale, 327-9283
- **Caldor's Inc.,** 400 Western Avenue, Brighton, 782-0502
- **Filene's Basement**, 450 Washington Street, Boston, 542-2011. The Basement opened in 1909, and this is where Boston's discount shopping began. You can find absolutely amazing markdowns but you must prepare yourself for this environment: the Basement is not

for the fainthearted. You may have to stop in more than once before you succeed in buying something, but eventually you'll become one of the converted. Management has recently added fitting rooms so you're less likely to find people trying on clothes in the aisles, but the no-holds-barred atmosphere still prevails. The Basement carries mostly clothing and shoes, but the second level has housewares, linen and home decorations.

- **Macy's Basement**, 450 Washington Street, Boston, 357-3000. Right across the street from Filene's Basement, the atmosphere here is much more subdued, but you can still find great bargains.
- **Macy's Furniture Gallery**, Shoppers World Mall, Routes 9 and 30, Framingham, 508-650-6000. The store is a little farther away, but it may well be worth your while. Macy's sends its leftover merchandise here where it is marked down even further. You can find electronic equipment, beds and furniture.
- **Kmart**, 77 Middlesex Avenue, Somerville, 628-9500
- **Marshalls**, 275 Needham, Newton Upper Falls, 964-4987; 455 Arsenal Street, Watertown, 923-1004; 500 Boylston Street, Boston, 262-6066

MALLS

- **Arsenal Mall/Watertown Mall**, 550 Arsenal Street, Watertown
- **Assembly Square Mall**, 133 Middlesex Avenue, Somerville
- **The Atrium**, 300 Boylston Street (Route 9), Newton
- **Burlington Mall**, 1 Burlington Mall Road, Burlington
- **Cambridgeside Galleria**, 100 Cambridgeside Place, Cambridge
- **Charles Square**, 20 University Road, Cambridge, 491-5282
- **The Mall at Chestnut Hill**, 199 Boylston Street (Route 9), Chestnut Hill
- **Colonial Shopping Mall**, 85 River Street, Waltham
- **Copley Place**, one block from Copley Square on Dartmouth or Huntington
- **Fresh Pond Shopping Center**, 186 Alewife Brook Parkway, Cambridge
- **Meadow Glen Mall**, 3850 Mystic Valley Parkway, Medford
- **Porter Exchange Mall**, 1815 Mass. Ave., Cambridge
- **Shops at the Prudential**, 800 Boylston Street, Boston

BEDS AND BEDDING

Locals call Cambridge the futon capital of Massachusetts. Department and furniture stores also carry beds and bedding. You can check the Yellow Pages under "Mattresses" and "Futons." In the meantime here's a list to get you started.

- **Bedworks - The Futon Shop**, 15 Western Avenue (near Central Square), Cambridge, 547-6000
- **Big John's Sleep Factory**, 121 First Street, Cambridge, 876-6344
- **Futon Express**, 1030 Mass. Ave., Cambridge, 547-2300
- **The Futon Outlet**, 360 Mystic Avenue, Somerville, 776-9429
- **Heartwood Furniture**, 1013 Mass. Ave., Cambridge, 547-1213
- **Home Design**, 1033 Mass. Ave., Cambridge, 354-2525
- **Jennifer Convertibles**, 1524 VFW Parkway, West Roxbury, 325-4891; 1 Porter Square, Cambridge, 661-0200
- **Jordan's Furniture**, 289 Moody Street, Waltham, 894-6100
- **Sleep-A-Rama**, has many locations in the Boston metro area. Check the Yellow Pages for listing.
- **Sofa and Futon Warehouse**, 244 Brighton Avenue, Allston, 254-5040

CAMERAS, ELECTRONICS, APPLIANCES

- **Advantage Kitchens**, 56 Ransdale Street (Route 9), Newton, 527-6633
- **Ashmont Discount Home Center**, 4165 Washington Street, Roslindale, 327-2080
- **Cambridge Camera Exchange**, 727 Revere Beach Parkway, Revere, 781-284-2300
- **Commonwealth Builder's Supply**, 375 Boylston Street, Brookline, 731-1800
- **General Photographic Supply Co.**, 71-73 Canal Street, Boston, 742-7070
- **Mystic Appliance**, 135 Cambridge Street, Charlestown, 242-9679
- **Shermans**, 11 Bromfield Street, Boston, 482-9610

CARPETS AND RUGS

- **Able Rug Company**, 20 Franklin Street, Allston, 782-5010
- **C & S Carpet**, 756 Dudley Street, Dorchester, 524-7479
- **Lechmere Rug Company**, 200 Monsignor O'Brien Highway, Cambridge, 876-9700

COMPUTER EQUIPMENT

The list of computer dealers in the Yellow Pages seems endless. A good place to begin your mission is to look through the mail order catalogs from places like MacWarehouse. Once you've got some ideas about what kind of computer you'd like and how much you want to spend, check the Yellow Pages for authorized dealers of the brand you think you want. Mail order places may seem cheaper but you should always factor service into the equation.

FOOD SHOPPING

Boston's surprisingly large immigrant population means you can find all sorts of delicious international delicacies here. If you're interested in Chinese or southeast Asian food markets try Chinatown and Allston/Brighton. If you're looking for Italian foodstuffs try the North End. Armenian and Greek? Go to Watertown. You'll find seafood everywhere, especially in the North End, the Haymarket area and Chinatown. If you're searching for a Japanese supermarket try the Porter Exchange Mall.

Major grocery store chains in metro Boston are **Star Market** and **Stop & Shop**.

- **Star Market**, 1065 Commonwealth Avenue, Allston, 783-5878; 800 Boylston Street, Prudential Center, 262-4688; 370 Western Avenue, Brighton, 787-5266; 1717 Beacon Street, Brookline, 566-1802; 699 Mt. Auburn Street, Cambridge, 876-1450; 49 White Street, Cambridge, 492-5566; 1 Boylston Street (Route 9), Chestnut Hill, 566-5858; 275 Beacon Street, Somerville, 354-7023; 299 Broadway, Somerville, 776-7733; 74 McGrath Highway, Somerville, 625-4070; 75 Spring Street, West Roxbury, 327-0564; 33 Austin Street, Newton, 964- 6825; 90 River Street, Waltham, 781-891-9816; 1070 Lexington Avenue, Waltham, 781-891-0615
- **Stop & Shop**, 905 Mass. Ave., Arlington, 781-646-3625; 181

Cambridge Street, Boston, 742-6094; 15 Westland Avenue, Boston, 267-9044; 15 Washington Street, Brighton, 566-0934; 155 Harvard Street, Brookline, 566-4559; 200 Alewife Brook Parkway, Cambridge, 547-2133; 200 Boylston Street, Newton, 244-6444; 950 American Legion Highway, Roslindale, 327-2160; 550 Arsenal Street, Watertown, 923-0527

- **Bread & Circus** is a local chain of full-service, supermarket-sized natural food stores that have to be seen to be believed. People from tropical climates drop by to visit the fruit displays when they're feeling homesick. Locations are at 115 Prospect Street in Cambridge, 492-0070; Fresh Pond Mall on the Alewife Parkway in Cambridge, 491-0040; 916 Walnut Street in Newton, 969-1141; 15 Washington Street in Brookline, 738-8187
- **Trader Joe's**, 727 Memorial Drive, Cambridge, 491-8582; 1317 Beacon Street in Brookline, 278-9997; 659 Worcester Road in Framingham, 508-935-2931; 958 Highland Avenue in Neeham Heights, 781-449-6993
- **The Harvest Cooperative Supermarkets**. The Cooperative still has two locations: 449 Cambridge Street, Allston, 787-1416; 581 Mass. Ave., Cambridge, 661-1580.

If you're hooked on organics the food coops and farmers markets are where you need to shop. Metro Boston offers a large number of area farmer's markets. For exact schedules call either your town hall or the Massachusetts Department of Food and Agriculture at 727-3018, ext. 175. The following is a partial listing:

- **Brookline Farmer's Market**, located near Coolidge Corner at the corner of Webster and Beacon Streets, runs from mid-June to the end of October on Thursday afternoons.
- **Cambridge Farmer's Market** at Central Square, located at the corner of Bishop Allen Drive and Norfolk Street, runs from mid-May to mid-November on Monday afternoons.
- **The Charles Square Farmer's Market** is next to Harvard Square in Cambridge. It runs from mid-June to mid-November on Sundays from 10 to 4.
- **The Copley Square Farmer's Market** is located along St. James Street. It starts in July, ends in late November and runs on Tuesdays and Fridays from 11 to 6.
- **Jamaica Plain Farmer's Market** is held in the Curtis Hall Municipal

Building parking lot where South and Centre street divide. It starts in mid-July, ends in late October and occurs on Tuesday afternoons.

- **Newton Farmer's Market** takes place at Cold Spring Park, 1200 Beacon Street in Auburndale. It starts in July, ends in late October and is open on Tuesday afternoons.
- **Quincy Farmer's Market** is held in the John Hancock parking lot in Quincy Center on Fridays from 11:30 a.m. to 5 p.m. from late June through October.
- **Roslindale Farmer's Market** is held at Taft Court between South and Corinth Streets in Roslindale Village. It is held on Saturdays from 9 to 1 beginning in mid-June and ending at the end of October.
- **Scollay Square** is another name for Government Center. This farmer's market is held on the City Hall Plaza on Monday and Wednesday afternoons from mid-July to mid-November.
- **Somerville's Farmer's Market** is held on Davis Square at Day and Herbert Streets. It runs on Wednesday afternoons from mid-June to late October.
- **Waltham's Farmer's Market** is held in the Embassy parking lot off Pine Street. Beginning in mid-June and ending in mid-October, this market is open Saturdays from 10 to 3.
- **Allandale Farm** is a working farm in Chestnut Hill located at 259 Allandale Road, 524-1531. It's open from May through December.
- Boston's famous **Haymarket** is not a farmer's market. Open on Fridays and Saturdays, the Haymarket is where wholesalers try to sell produce that they couldn't sell to supermarkets or other markets. Everyone should experience the Haymarket at least once, but keep your wits about you and carry lots of one dollar bills. If you can process that $4 case of strawberries as soon as you get home, you may feel that you've gotten quite a bargain. The Haymarket is a good place to go if you have something specific in mind, for example, a case of limes or lemons for a margarita party.

FURNITURE

Believe it or not, trash picking is a time-honored practice in Boston that stems from the biannual influx and outflow of students who streamline at an amazing rate before moving on. You can find brand new items that didn't fit in the dump truck on trash days. However, if trash picking is not for you, try one of the following stores and don't forget to refer to the Beds and Bedding section above.

- **Bernstein Furniture Co.**, 154 Harvard Avenue, Allston, 782-7972
- **Boston Paint and Supply Co.**, 151 Harvard Avenue, Allston, 254-1060
- **Choice Seating Gallery**, 1001 Mass. Ave., Cambridge, 492-2646
- **City Schemes**, 1050 Mass. Ave., Cambridge, 497-0707
- **Eastern Butcher Block**, 236 Wood Road, Braintree, Boston, 423-2173
- **Home Design**, 1033 Mass. Ave., Cambridge, 354-2525
- **Home Furniture**, 450 Providence Highway on Route 1, Dedham, 329-4770 and 454 Main Street, Malden, 397-1700
- **Maverick Designs**, Inc., 1117 Commonwealth Ave., Brighton, 783-0274
- **Sallet Furniture**, 44 Harvard Avenue, Allston, 782-1891
- **The Oak Gallery**, 2285 Mass. Ave., Cambridge, 492-8220

HARDWARE, PAINTS, WALLPAPER

You should be able to find a hardware store in your neighborhood no matter where you live. For your convenience, the Ace and True Value locations are listed below.

Ace Affiliates:

- **Ace Hardware City**, 656 Centre Street, Jamaica Plain, 983-5466
- **Inman Square Hardware, Inc.**, 1337 Cambridge Street, Cambridge, 491-3405
- **Model Hardware, Inc.**, 22 Harvard Avenue, Allston, 782-5131
- **Roslindale Hardware Supply**, 4407 Washington Street , Roslindale, 323-8639
- **R.W. Shattuck and Co.**, 24 Mill Street, Arlington,781- 643-0114
- **Tags Ace Hardware**, Porter Square Shopping Center, Cambridge, 868-7711

True Value Affiliates:

- **Aborn True Value Hardware**, 438 Harvard Street, Brookline, 277-4533
- **Atlas True Value**, 1871 Centre Street, West Roxbury, 325-9494

- **Charles Street Supply Co. & True Value**, 54 Charles Street, Boston, 367- 9046
- **Cleveland Circle Hardware Co.**, 1920 Beacon Street, Brookline, 734-6440
- **Dickson Brothers True Value**, 26 Brattle Street, Cambridge, 876-6760
- **Economy Hardware**, 1012-1024 Beacon Street, Brookline, 277-8811
- **Hillside Garden Supply Co.**, 280 Blanchard Road, Belmont, 489-0250
- **Nickerson Hardware Co., Inc.**, 121 Brighton Avenue, Allston, 782-3311
- **Parks Paint & Hardware**, 233 Newbury Street, Boston, 536-0913
- **Pills True Value Hardware**, 743 Mass. Ave., Cambridge, 876-8310
- **Salem Street True Value Hardware**, 89 Salem Street, Boston, 523-4759
- **Wanamaker Hardware**, 1298 Mass. Ave., Arlington,781-643-1900
- **Warren Electric and Hardware Supply**, 470 Tremont Street, Boston, 426-7525
- **Yumont Hardware**, 702 Centre Street, Jamaica Plain, 524-4572

HOUSEWARES

If you love to browse, you'll enjoy discovering the many talented artists who sell their unique housewares in small shops throughout the area. However, if you're in a rush to outfit your kitchen fast, you may want to try one of the following soup-to-nuts establishments.

- **China Fair**, 2100 Mass. Ave., Cambridge, 864-3050; 70 Needham Street, Newton, 332-1250
- **Crate and Barrel**, 48 Brattle Street, Cambridge, 876-6300; 1 Copley Place, Boston, 536-9400; 140 Faneuil Hall, Boston, 742-6025; The Mall at Chestnut Hill, Newton, 964-8400
- **Lechter's**, 100 Cambridgeside Place, Cambridge, 577-0353; 133 Middlesex Avenue, Somerville, 625-3454; Prudential Center Shoppes, Boston, 236-0798
- **Pottery Barn**, 1000 Mass. Ave., Cambridge, 492-8731; 122 Newbury Street, Boston, 536-9130

And don't forget the department stores.

SECOND-HAND SHOPPING

You just never know what you might find . . .

- **Amvets Thrift Store**, 80 Brighton Avenue, Allston, 562-0720
- **Beacon Hill Thrift Shop**, 15 Charles Street, Boston, 742-2323
- **Beth Israel Hospital Thrift Shop**, 25 Harvard Street, Brookline, 566-7016
- **Ernie's Thrift Shop**, 509 Columbus Avenue, Boston, no phone
- **Goodwill Bargain Basement**, 520 Mass. Ave., Cambridge, 868-6330; 230 Elm Street, Somerville, 628-3618; 708 Centre Street, Jamaica Plain, 983-5354
- **Hadassah Bargain Spot**, 1123 Commonwealth Avenue, Brighton, 254-8300
- **St. Vincent De Paul Thrift Store**, 1280 Washington Street, Boston, 542-0883, 50 Prospect Street, Cambridge, 547-6924; 297 Lowell Avenue, Newton, 969- 9520
- **Salvation Army Thrift Store**, 483 Broadway, Somerville, 395-9783
- **Thrift Shop of Boston**, 640 Centre Street, Jamaica Plain, 522-5676

SPORTING GOODS, BICYCLES, SKI EQUIPMENT

Boston's population stays fit in many ways.

- **Bicycle Bill**, 253 North Harvard Street, Allston, 783-5636
- **The Bicycle Exchange**, 2067 Mass. Ave., Cambridge, 864-1300
- **The Bicycle Workshop**, 259 Mass. Ave., Cambridge, 876-6555
- **Bill Rodgers Running Center**, Faneuil Hall, North Market Building, 723-5612
- **Bob Smith Sporting Goods**, 9 Spring Lane, Boston, 426-4440
- **Broadway Bicycle School**, 351 Broadway, Cambridge, 868-3392
- **City Sports**, 480 Boylston Street, Boston, 267-3900; 168 Mass. Ave., Boston, 236-2222; 1035 Commonwealth Avenue, Boston, 782-5022; 105 First Street, East Cambridge, 868-9232; 16 Dunster Street, Cambridge, 868-9232; 37 Boylston Street, Chestnut Hill, 566-0220
- **Charles River Sports**, 151 Merrimac Street, Boston, 720-1872
- **Eastern Mountain Sports**, 1041 Commonwealth Avenue, Boston , 254-4250

- **Nevada Bob's Golf Mart**, 2 Liberty Square, Boston, 695-1971
- **Play It Again Sports**, 626 Washington Street, Dedham, 781-320-8114
- **REI (Recreational Equipment, Inc.)**, 279 Salem Street, Reading, 944-5103
- **Ski Market**, 860 Commonwealth Avenue, Boston, 731-6100 (not just skis)
- **The Ski Warehouse**, 372 Main Street, Watertown, 924-4643
- **Bob Smith's Wilderness House**, 1048 Commonwealth Avenue, Boston, 277- 5858

Finding the right spiritual connection isn't always easy. Just relax and don't be disappointed if you don't get it right the first time. *The Newcomer's Handbook®* can't offer a complete listing of places of worship in metro Boston—not even the Yellow Pages does—but we give you a place to start. If your spirituality is of a non-traditional nature, check the listings under interdenominational, nondenominational and other denominations.

AFRICAN METHODIST EPISCOPAL AND EPISCOPAL ZION

- **Bethel African Methodist Episcopal Church**, 215 Forest Hills, Jamaica Plain, 524-4311
- **Columbus Avenue AME Zion Church**, 600 Columbus Avenue, Boston 266- 2758
- **Friends of the Haitian Church**, 41 Moultrie, Dorchester, 288-2289
- **St. Paul's AME Church**, 85 Bishop Richard Allen Drive, Cambridge, 661-1110

APOSTOLIC

- **Christ Tabernacle Church**, 401 Norfolk Street, Dorchester, 265-5930
- **Holy Trinity Armenian Apostolic Church of Greater Boston**, 145 Brattle Street, Cambridge, 354-0632
- **St. Stephen's Armenian Apostolic Church of Greater Boston**, 38 Elton Avenue, Watertown, 924-9860
- **United Emmanuel Holiness Church**, 65 Windsor, Roxbury, 442-4183

ASSEMBLIES OF GOD

- **Assembleia De Deus**, 50 Bennington, East Boston, 561-0602
- **Boston Worship Center**, 9 Salutation Street, Boston (North End), 723-2226
- **Cross Roads Evangelical Church**, 51 Lexington Street, Belmont, 489-4959
- **Church In The City Assemblies of God**, 1644 Dorchester Avenue, 825-9425

BAHA'I

- **Baha'i Center of Boston**, 595 Albany Street, Boston, 695-3500
- **Baha'i Faith**, 68 High Street, Malden, 781-322-2662

BAPTIST

- **The Baptist Church in Brookline-United Parish**, 210 Harvard Street, Brookline, 277-6860
- **Beth Eden Baptist Church**, 84 Maple Street, Waltham, 781-899-4674
- **Community Baptist Church**, 31 College Avenue, Somerville, 625-6523
- **Concord Baptist Church**, 190 Warren Avenue, Boston, 266-8062
- **Cornerstone Baptist Church**, 54 Brighton Street, Belmont, 489-2498
- **First Baptist Church of Arlington**, 819 Mass. Ave., Arlington, 781-643-3024
- **First Baptist Church of Jamaica Plain**, 633 Centre Street, Jamaica Plain, 524-2420
- **Hill Memorial Baptist Church**, 279 North Harvard Street, Brighton, 782-4524
- **Roslindale Baptist Church**, 52 Cummins Highway, Roslindale, 327-5262
- **South End Neighborhood Church of Emmanuel**, 2 San Juan, Boston, 262-0900

CATHOLIC

- **Archdiocese of Boston**, 127 Lake Street, Brighton, 254-2610
- **Hispanic Apostolate**, 76 Union Parkway, Boston, 357-5858
- **Holy Name Church**, 521 West Roxbury Parkway, West Roxbury, 323-9541
- **Immaculate Conception**, 45 Matignon Road, Cambridge, 547-3077
- **Paulist Center and Chapel**, 5 Park Street, Boston, 742-4460
- **St. Anthony Shrine**, 100 Arch Street, Boston, 542-6440
- **St. Anthony's Parish**, 12 Properzi Way, Somerville, 625-4530
- **St. Francis De Sales**, 303 Bunker Hill, Charlestown, 242-0147
- **St. Francis Prudential Chapel**, Prudential Center, Boston, 437-7117
- **St. Mary's Parish**, 46 Winthrop Street, Charlestown, 242-2196
- **St. Roger and St. Mary Chapel**, 95 Rockland, West Roxbury, 327-4546

CHRISTIAN SCIENCE

- **First Church of Christ Scientist**, The Mother Church Headquarters and General Offices, 175 Huntington Avenue, Boston, 450-2000
- **Cambridge First Church of Christ Scientist**, 13 Waterhouse Street, 354-2866; 386 Main Street, 749-1946; 707 Washington Street, 762-4135
- **Somerville First Church of Christ Scientist**, 21-A College Avenue, 625-6340; 114 Church, 729-5856

CHURCH OF CHRIST

- **Church of Christ in Roxbury**, 81 Walnut Avenue, Roxbury, 442-5826
- **Dorchester Church of Christ**, 179 Glenway, Dorchester, 282-7900

CHURCH OF GOD

- **Church of God of Prophecy**, 270 Warren Street, Roxbury, 427-7766
- **Church of God of Prophecy**, 190 Harvard Street, Cambridge, 661-3660

Church of the Nazarene
- **Church of the Nazarene of Cambridge**, 234 Franklin Street, Cambridge, 354-5065
- **Church of the Nazarene of Somerville**, 52 Russell Street, Somerville, 628-1898
- **Community Church of the Nazarene**, 1450 Trapelo Road, Waltham,
  781-890-7629

COMMUNITY

- **Chinese Evangelical Church of Metro-Boston**, 41 Quint Avenue, Brighton, 254-4039
- **Community Church of Boston**, 565 Boylston Street, Boston, 266-6710
- **Watertown Evangelical Church**, 182 Arlington Street, Watertown, 924-1778

CONGREGATIONAL

- **Armenian Memorial Congregational Church**, 32 Bigelow Avenue, Watertown, 923-0498
- **Brighton Evangelical Congregational Church**, 404 Washington Street, Brighton, 254-4046
- **Central Congregational Church**, 218 Walnut Street, Newton, 244-5395
- **First Armenian Church**, 380 Concord Avenue, Belmont, 484-4779
- **First Church in Cambridge**, 11 Garden Street, Cambridge, 876-5829
- **First Church of Somerville**, 95 College Avenue, Somerville, 625-6485
- **First Congregational Church of Waltham**, 730 Main Street, Waltham, 781-899-3891
- **Park Street Church**, One Park Street, Boston, 523-3383
- **Roslindale Congregational Church**, 25 Cummins Highway, West Roxbury, 323-8302
- **Union Church in Waban**, 14 Collins Road, Newton, 527-6221

EASTERN ORTHODOX

- **Eastern Orthodox Church of the Holy Resurrection**, 64 Harvard Street, Allston, 787-7625
- **Greek Orthodox Church**, 25 Bigelow Avenue, Watertown, 924-9592
- **Greek Orthodox Church Dormition**, 29 Central Street, Somerville, 625-2222
- **Greek Orthodox Church of Arlington**, 735 Mass. Ave. Arlington, 781-646- 0705
- **Greek Orthodox Church St. Constantine and Helen**, 14 Magazine Street, Cambridge, 354-8323
- **Greek Orthodox Church St. John The Baptist**, 15 Union Park, Boston, 536-5692
- **Russian Orthodox Church of Epiphany**, 963 South Street, Roslindale, 327-3663

EPISCOPAL

- **All Saints Parish of Brookline**, 1773 Beacon Street, Brookline, 738-1810
- **Cathedral Church of St. Paul**, 138 Tremont Street, Boston, 482-5800
- **Christ Church of Cambridge**, Zero Garden, Cambridge, 876-0200
- **Christ Episcopal Church**, 66 Fellsway West, Somerville, 628-4519
- **Church of Good Shepherd**, 1671 Beacon Street, Newton, 244-4028; 9 Russell Avenue, Watertown, 924-9420
- **Church of Our Savior**, 21 Marathon Street, Arlington, 781-648-5962
- **Emmanuel Church of Boston**, 15 Newbury Street, Boston, 536-3355
- **Old North Church**, 193 Salem Street, Boston, 523-6676
- **St. Luke's and St. Margaret's Church**, 5 St. Lukes Road, Brighton, 782-2029
- **Trinity Church**, Copley Square, Boston, 536-0944

FRIENDS

- **Beacon Hill Friends House**, 6 Chestnut Street, Boston, 227-9118

- **Friends Meeting At Cambridge**, 5 Longfellow Park, Cambridge, 876-6883

INTERDENOMINATIONAL

- **Chinese Christian Church of New England**, 1835 Beacon Street, Brookline, 232-8652
- **Emmanuel Gospel Center**, 2 San Juan, Boston, 262-4567
- **New Life Church**, 39 Fordham Road, Brighton, 562-0220
- **Unification Church of Boston**, 46 Beacon Street, Boston, 723-6234
- **United Parish in Brookline**, 210 Harvard Street, Brookline, 277-6860

ISLAMIC

- **Islamic Center of New England**, 470 South Street, Quincy, 479-8341
- **Masjid Al-Quran**, 35 Intervale, Dorchester, 445-8070

JEHOVAH'S WITNESSES

- **Jamaica Plain Spanish Congregation of Jehovah's Witness**, 10 Kingsboro Park, Jamaica Plain, 522-1142
- **Jehovah's Witness Congregation of Jamaica Plain**, 236 Chestnut Avenue, Jamaica Plain, 522-7521
- **Kingdom Hall of Jehovah's Witnesses**, 49 Brooksdale Road, Brighton, 782-1766

JEWISH — CONSERVATIVE

- **Congregation Kehillath Israel**, 384 Harvard Street, Brookline, 277-9155
- **Congregation Mishkan Tefila**, 300 Hammond Pond Parkway, Chestnut Hill, 332-7770
- **Temple Adas-Hadrath Israel**, 28 Arlington Street, Hyde Park, 354-2661
- **Temple Beth Israel**, 25 Harvard Street, Waltham, 781-894-5146
- **Temple Beth Zion**, 1566 Beacon Street, Brookline, 566-8171
- **Temple B'nai Brith**, 201 Central Street, Somerville, 625-0333
- **Temple B'nai Moshe**, 1845 Commonwealth Avenue, Brighton,

254-3620
- **Temple Emmanuel**, 385 Ward Street, Newton, 332-5770
- **Temple Reyim**, 1860 Washington Street, Newton, 527-2410

JEWISH — ORTHODOX

- **Congregation Beth-El Ateveth Israel**, 561 Ward Street, Newton Centre, 244-7305
- **Congregation Chai Odom**, 77 Englewood Avenue, Brookline, 734-5359
- **Congregation Georgetown Synagogue**, 412 Georgetown Drive, Hyde Park, 361-8212
- **Congregation Kadimah-Toras Moshe**, 113 Washington Street, Brighton, 254-1333
- **Lubavitch Shul of Brighton**, 239 Chestnut Hill Avenue, Brighton, 782-8340
- **Sephardic Community of Greater Boston**, 74 Corey Road, Brookline, 232-7979

JEWISH — REFORM

- **Beth-El Temple Center**, 2 Concord Avenue, Belmont, 484-6668
- **Congregation Adath Israel (Temple Israel)**, 260 Riverway, Boston, 566-3960
- **Temple Beth Avodah**, 45 Puddingstone Lane, Newton Centre, 527-0045
- **Temple Ohabei Shalom**, 1187 Beacon Street, Brookline, 277-6610
- **Temple Shalom**, 175 Temple Street, Newton, 332-9550
- **Temple Sinai**, Charles Street and Sewell Avenue (Coolidge Corner), Brookline, 277-5888

LUTHERAN

- **Bethlehem Lutheran Church**, 5 Cliftondale, Roslindale, 325-4559
- **Christ Lutheran Church**, 597 Belmont Street, Belmont, 484-4352
- **Faith Lutheran Church**, 311 Broadway Street, Cambridge, 354-0414
- **First Lutheran Church of Boston**, 299 Berkeley Street, Boston, 536-8851
- **First Lutheran Church of Waltham**, corner of Eddy and Weston, Waltham, 781-893-6563

- **Lutheran Church of Newton,** 1310 Centre Street, Newton, 332-3893
- **St. Paul Lutheran Church,** 929 Concord Turnpike, Arlington, 781-646-7773
- **University Lutheran Church,** 66 Winthrop Street, Cambridge, 876-3256

METHODIST

- **Bethany United Methodist Church,** 100 Cummins Highway, Roslindale, 327-2532
- **Korean Methodist Church of Boston,** 68 College Avenue, Somerville, 629-2322
- **United Methodist Church of Newton,** 430 Walnut Street, Street, 244-0275

NONDENOMINATIONAL

- **Covenant Church,** 9 Westminster Avenue, Arlington, 781-646-9027
- **Grace Christian Fellowship Church,** 858 Hyde Park Avenue, Hyde Park, 364-3344
- **Jesus,** 65 Chestnut Hill Avenue, Brighton, 782-1720
- **The Lord's Gathering,** 4 Bangor Road, West Roxbury, 325-0442
- **Mt. Olive Temple of Christ,** 234 Norfolk, Dorchester, 288-8830
- **Mount Auburn Gospel Center,** 226 Mt. Auburn Street, Watertown, 924-7696
- **New England Center of Tao,** Waltham, 781-899-7120
- **Summit Lighthouse,** 1082 Walnut Street, Newton, 965-5395

OTHER DENOMINATIONS

- **Aquarian Truth Center of Light,** 99 Myrtle Street, Boston, 723-9100
- **Dharmadhatu Buddist Meditation Center,** 515 Centre Street, Newton, 965-2827
- **First Spiritual Temple,** 16 Monmouth, Brookline, 566-7639
- **Ramakrishna Vedanta Society Church,** 58 Deerfield, Boston, 536-5320

PRESBYTERIAN

- **Church of the Covenant**, 67 Newbury Street, Boston, 266-7480
- **Clarendon Hill Presbyterian Church**, 155 Powderhouse Boulevard, Somerville, 625-4823
- **First Presbyterian Church of Waltham**, 34 Adler Street, Waltham, 781-893-3087
- **First Reformed Presbyterian Church**, 53 Antrim Street, Cambridge, 864-3185
- **Korean Church of Boston**, 32 Harvard, Brookline, 739-2663
- **Korean Presbyterian Church in Boston**, 218 Walnut Street, Newton, 964-7964
- **Newton Presbyterian Church**, 75 Vernon Street, Newton, 332-9255
- **United Presbyterian Church of Cambridge**, 1418 Cambridge Street, Cambridge, 354-3151

UNITARIAN — UNIVERSALIST

- **First Church in Belmont**, 404 Concord Avenue, Belmont, 484-1054
- **First Church in Jamaica Plain**, 6 Eliot Street, Jamaica Plain, 524-1634
- **First Parish in Brookline**, 382 Walnut Street, Brookline, 566-1933
- **First Parish in Cambridge**, 3 Church Street, Cambridge, 876-7772
- **First Parish in Waltham**, 50 Church Street, Waltham, 781-893-6240
- **First & Second Church in Boston**, 66 Marlborough Street, Boston, 267-6730
- **First Unitarian Society in Newton**, 1326 Washington Street, Newton, 527-3203
- **King's Chapel**, 58 Tremont Street, Boston, 523-1749
- **Theodore Parker Unitarian Church**, 1859 Centre Street, West Roxbury, 325-4439
- **Unitarian First Parish in Watertown**, 35 Church Street, Watertown, 924-6143

UNITED CHURCH OF CHRIST

- **Allston Congregational Church**, 41 Quint Avenue, Brighton, 254-2920
- **Brighton Congregational Church**, 404 Washington Street,

Brighton, 254-4046
- **Central Congregational Church**, 85 Seaverns Avenue, Jamaica Plain, 524-3343
- **Harvard Church-United Parish**, 210 Harvard Avenue, Brookline, 277-6860
- **Old South Church**, 645 Boylston Street, Boston, 536-1970
- **Park Avenue Congregational Church**, 50 Paul Revere Road, Arlington, 781-643-8680

UNITED METHODIST

- **Belmont United Methodist Church**, 421 Common Street, Belmont, 489-0730
- **Calvary United Methodist Church**, 300 Mass. Ave., Arlington, 781-646-8679
- **Church of All Nations - Morgan Memorial**, 333 Tremont Street, Boston, 357-5777
- **College Avenue Methodist Church**, 14 Chapel Street, Somerville, 776-4172
- **Community United Methodist Church**, 519 Washington Street, Brighton, 787-1868
- **Grace United Methodist Church**, 56 Magazine Street, Cambridge, 864-1123
- **Immanuel United Methodist Church**, 545 Moody Street, Waltham, 781-893-7250
- **St. Mark's Methodist - United Parish**, 210 Harvard, Brookline, 277-6860
- **United Parish of Auburndale**, 64 Hancock, Newton, 964-8516

UNITY

- **Unity-Christ's Church Longwood**, Colchester, Brookline, 232-4548
- **Unity Church of God**, service at 1950 Mass. Ave., Cambridge, 536-2207

B oston was once known as the "Athens of America," and its cultural scene still strives to uphold this weighty moniker. The Boston Symphony Orchestra and the Boston Ballet offer world-class entertainment. Modern dance is also well represented. Dance Umbrella hosts Mark Morris' dance troupe for two months every year and stages other performances as well.

The theater district usually sells out nightly and small theater groups are constantly on the prowl for new places to stage their productions. You can hear a chamber orchestra, brass quartet or jazz recital almost any night of the week at one of the area's music schools. The popular music scene in both Boston and Cambridge is vibrantly alive. The area's museums and galleries strive for excellence in their exhibitions and concerts.

Boston's lecture circuit is unsurpassed. And where else but Boston would the bar association stage a trial in which representatives of the local academic scene and Great Britain's Lord Burford presented conflicting evidence in their attempt to prove who really wrote Shakespeare's plays?

Don't let these opportunities pass you by. After all, isn't this at least part of the reason why you moved to Boston? As the weekend approaches check your most accessible sources — the newspapers. Most of the area's weekly local newspapers list events but the dailies (*The Globe* and the *Herald*) produce special pull-out entertainment guides each week. *The Globe*'s, called "Calendar," comes with the Thursday paper and the *Herald*'s, called "Scene," arrives on Friday. Both papers offer extensive entertainment sections on Sundays as well. An additional source is *the Phoenix*, a weekly paper pretty much devoted to getting out and about.

All of these guides will alert you to square dancing opportunities, lectures, theater openings and ongoing shows, dinner theater, concerts, movies, openings at galleries and museums, nightclubs, and nature walks. Also, leaf through a *Harvard Gazette* if you get the chance.

There are a couple of hotline numbers and ticket sources that you should know about:

- **Arts Boston**, 100 Boylston Street, 423-4454, is partially funded by the Massachusetts Cultural Council. They sell discount tickets through mail order, letting you know what's available with their newsletter Artsmail. Call to get on their mailing list.
- **Artscall**, 349-4394, gives you a listing of Cambridge events, performances and exhibits.
- **BOSTIX** is run by Arts Boston out of a booth at Faneuil Hall Marketplace and a booth is now located at Copley Square. You can find half-price, day-of-show tickets and other bargains. Cash only.
- **Boston Jazz Line**, 787-9700, offers weekly information about area jazz shows.
- **Boston Symphony Orchestra** offers 24-hour-a-day concert information. Call 266-2378.

MUSIC

SYMPHONIC, CHORAL, OPERA, CHAMBER

BOSTON SYMPHONY ORCHESTRA AND THE BOSTON POPS

A music-lover and philanthropist named Henry Lee Higginson saw the need for a Boston-based symphony orchestra in 1881. Thus, the Boston Symphony Orchestra (BSO) was born, and by the turn of the century it had moved to its current home, **Symphony Hall**, located at 301 Mass. Ave., Boston. Acoustically, Symphony Hall is considered one of the world's finest concert halls.

The Boston Pops began in 1885, first known as Boston Promenade, then as Popular Concerts, and finally as our beloved Boston Pops. The Pops evolved out of Higginson's desire to keep the BSO musicians occupied during the summer. With a winter season only, many musicians were forced to tour Europe in the summers to stay financially solvent. Sometimes they didn't return to Boston.

Today, the Pops orchestra and the BSO no longer share musicians — they are completely separate entities. The BSO and musical director Seiji Ozawa travel to Tanglewood, located in Lenox, Massachusetts, each summer for concerts in this glorious Berkshire setting. Meanwhile, the Boston Pops takes over Symphony Hall from May through July: chairs are replaced with small tables resulting in a festive, more night-clubby atmosphere. Each July, the Pops presents a series of free concerts at the Hatch Shell on the Esplanade.

For **Pops tickets** call 266-1492.

BSO tickets are available in a number of ways:

- **Mail**. Send orders which include a check and a self-addressed, stamped envelope to the Symphony Hall Box Office, Symphony Hall, 301 Mass. Ave., Boston, 02115.
- **Phone**. Charge ticket orders by phone through SymphonyCharge at 266-1200. You can also reserve your tickets through SymphonyCharge and send in your payment by check. There is a handling fee for each ticket ordered by phone. In the front of the Yellow Pages there is a floor plan of Symphony Hall in the front section.
- **In person**. The Box Office is open from 10:00 a.m. to 6:00 p.m., Monday through Saturday. The Box Office is also open during intermission on concert nights.
- **Fax**. Symphony Hall Box Office's fax number is 638-9247. Make sure you include all of your credit card information. There is also a handling fee for each ticket ordered by fax.
- A limited number of **rush tickets** are made available on the day of the show for concerts held on Friday afternoon and Tuesday and Thursday nights. These tickets are inexpensive (less than $10) and are sold one per person at the Mass. Ave. entrance beginning at 5:00 p.m. on Tuesdays and Thursdays and 9:00 a.m. on Fridays.
- Another inexpensive option is to attend one of the BSO's **open rehearsals** on certain Wednesday nights and Thursday mornings throughout the season; these are the final rehearsals before BSO concerts. Call the concert line (266-2378) to find out dates and times. Seating is unreserved.

NEW ENGLAND CONSERVATORY (NEC) AND JORDAN HALL

New England Conservatory, in existence for over 120 years, graduates prize-winning musicians, some of whom have nation-wide concert tours even before graduation. Musicians can earn both undergraduate and graduate degrees here. The school hosts over 400 concerts by faculty, students and guests at varying locations on campus and most of them are free.

NEC's **Jordan Hall** is on the National Register of Historic Places and boasts an acoustically superior performance facility. Over 100 free concerts are given at this hall each year by New England Conservatory students and faculty. The hall also hosts a number of performances by the **Boston Philharmonic (868-6696)**, **Handel & Haydn Society (262-1815)**, **Boston Gay Men's Chorus (247-2462)**, **Greater Boston Youth Symphony Orchestra (353-3348)** and **Boston Baroque (641-1310)**. The hall seats 1,000 and is located at the corner of Huntington Avenue and Gainsborough Street, Boston.

- **Jordan Hall Ticket Information**, 536-2412
- **New England Conservatory Concert Information**, 262-1120, ext.700

THE BOSTON LYRIC OPERA

The opera's offices are located at 114 State Street, but performances are usually at the **Emerson Majestic Theater** located at 219 Tremont Street. The company stages six productions each season.

- **Boston Lyric Opera information**, 248-8811
- **Emerson Majestic Theatre Box Office**, 578-8785

THE OPERA COMPANY OF BOSTON

The opera has not staged a production since the early 1990s. But there is an opportunity for parents to introduce their children to the wonders of opera through **Opera New England.** It presents one-hour versions of operas for children and families in the spring as a way to help youngsters gain an appreciation of the art. Call 451-6464.

BOSTON CAMERATA

This ensemble presents Medieval, Renaissance and early Baroque vocal and instrumental concerts at various locations around the city. On occasion they also perform 18th and 19th century American folk music. Call 262-2092 for information.

MUSIC – CONTEMPORARY

There are many exceptions to the following rule, but Boston's club scene is split among four key areas: **Harvard Avenue in Allston/Brighton**, the **North Station area** in downtown Boston, **Kenmore Square/ Landsdowne** Street, and **Central Square** in Cambridge. The following clubs feature mostly local and New England based acts. They also book up-and-coming national musicians who are touring smaller venues.

REGGAE, FUNK, WORLD BEAT, LATIN RHYTHMS, ETC.

Some of the following are gritty pubs and some are glitzy nightclubs that offer international music (live and recorded) on certain nights. Call to find out what's happening.

- **Bill's Bar**, 5.5 Landsdown Street, Boston, 421-9678, Reggae on Sundays
- **Caribbean Cultural Center**, 1000 Blue Hill Drive, Dorchester, 436-8629, 436-9246
- **Europa**, 51 Stuart Street, Boston, 482-3939
- **Kay's Oasis**, 1125 Blue Hill Avenue, Dorchester, 436-9566
- **Local 186**, 186 Harvard Avenue, Allston, 351-2608, Thursdays
- **The Middle East**, 472 Mass. Ave. (Central Square), Cambridge, 864-3278
- **Paradise**, 967 Commonwealth Avenue, Boston, 351-2582
- **Roxy**, 279 Tremont Street, Boston, 227-ROXY
- **The Western Front**, 343 Western Avenue, Cambridge, 492-7772
- **Windsor Cricket Club**, 327 Talbot Avenue, Dorchester, 436-9234

ROCK, GRUNGE, METAL, TRASH, SKA, ETC.

Most of the places listed above and some of the places listed under Jazz and Blues also fall into this category on certain nights. The following spots specialize, but also check the nightclubs section below.

- **The Beanpot**, 150 Canal Street, Boston, 722-9321
- **Blackbird Baking Company**, 1032 Commonwealth Avenue, Boston, 739-9755
- **Christopher's**, 1920 Mass. Ave., Cambridge, 876-5405
- **The Middle East**, 472 Mass. Ave. 864-3278
- **Nameless Coffeehouse**, 3 Church Street, Cambridge, 864-1630
- **Passim Coffee Shop**, 47 Palmer Street, Cambridge, 492-7679
- **The Rathskellar (The "Rat")**, 528 Commonwealth Avenue

(Kenmore Square), Boston, 536-2750
- **The Tam**, 299 Harvard Street, Brookline, 277-0982
- **Toad**, 1920 Mass. Ave. (Porter Square), Cambridge, 497-4950
- **TT the Bear's**, 10 Brookline Street (Central Square), Cambridge, 492-0082

JAZZ AND BLUES

- **Berklee College of Music and Berklee Performance Center**. This 1,200 seat performance hall, located at the Berklee College of Music on 136 Mass. Ave. in Boston, hosts jazz concerts. The box office phone number is 266-7455.
- **Regattabar**, Charles Hotel, 1 Bennett Street, Cambridge, 937-4020
- **Scullers Jazz Club**, Guest Quarters Suite Hotel, 400 Soldiers Field Road, 783-0090
- **Willow Jazz Club**, 699 Broadway (Ball Square), Somerville, 623-9874
- **House of Blues**, 96 Winthrop Street, Cambridge, 491-BLUE
- **Harper's Ferry**, 158 Brighton Avenue, Allston, 254-7380
- **Wally's Cafe**, 427 Mass. Ave., Boston, 424-1408
- **Johnny D's**, 17 Holland (Davis Square), Somerville, 776-2004
- **Sacco's**, 96 School Street, Watertown, 924-9804
- **Ryles**, 212 Hampshire, Cambridge, 876-9330

IRISH AND CELTIC

- **O'Leary's**, 1010 Beacon Street, Brookline, 734-0049
- **The Harp**, 85 Causeway Street, Boston, 742-1010
- **The Black Rose**, 160 State Street, Boston, 742-2286
- **The Kells**, 161 Brighton Avenue, Brighton, 782-9082

NIGHTCLUBS

The following clubs are medium to medium large. They are roomy enough to handle well-known national acts as well as those that have just begun to make a name for themselves. On nights with no live acts they play a lot of loud dance music. Most have a dress code.

- **Avalon**, 15 Landsdowne Street, Boston, 262-2424
- **Axis**, 13 Landsdowne Street, Boston, 262-2437
- **Bill's Bar**, 5 Landsdowne Street, Boston, 421-9678
- **Buzz Boston/Europa**, 51 Stuart Street, Boston, 482-3939
- **Karma Club**, 9 Landsdowne Street, Boston, 421-9595
- **Mama Kins**, 36 Landsdowne Street, Boston, 536-2100
- **Man Ray**, 21 Brookline Street, (Central Square), Cambridge, 864-0400
- **Roxy**, 279 Tremont Street, Boston, 338-7699
- **Karma Club**, 9 Landsdowne Street, Boston, 421-9595
- **The Big Easy Bar**, One Boylston Place, Boston, 351-7000

CONCERT HALLS, STADIUMS, ARENAS

- **Fleet Center**, Causeway Street, Boston, 624-1000
- **Orpheum Theatre**, Hamilton Place, Boston, 482-0652
- **Foxboro Stadium**, Route 1, Foxboro, event line - 508-543-3900, tickets - 800-543-1776
- **Worcester Centrum**, 50 Foster, Worcester, 508-931-2000

DANCE

PERFORMANCE DANCE

THE BOSTON BALLET
Founded nearly thirty years ago, this ballet company and its ballet school enjoy a reputation as one of the country's finest. The Boston Ballet performs both full-length classics and modern works.

The Boston Ballet performs at the **Wang Center for the Performing Arts**, a hall known for its luxurious 1920's architecture. For tickets:
- **The Boston Ballet**, 695-6950
- **The Wang Center for the Performing Arts**, 482-9393
- **Ticketmaster**, 931-2000

DANCE UMBRELLA
New England's most active contemporary dance company, Dance Umbrella stages and/or presents dancing from all over the world, all

through the year. Performances are year-round and take place all over the city. Call 482-7570 for information.

DANCE COLLECTIVE
A contemporary dance company that performs in unusual locations such as train stations and malls as well as a number of area theaters. Call 326-4822 for information.

HARVARD SUMMER DANCE CENTER
The center offers workshops and courses as well as performances and lectures each summer. They usually present at least one free show each year at the Hatch Memorial Shell. Call 495-5535 for information.

PARTICIPATORY DANCE

Located at 1950 Mass. Ave. in Cambridge, the **Folk Arts Center of New England** hosts participatory dance events each week. They teach traditional ethnic dances and publish a bi-monthly calendar of local dance events. Call 491-6084 for information.

- **Movement Collective Studio**, 23 Main Street (Watertown Square), Watertown, 924-7276 sponsors **Dance Friday**, a smoke-free, alcohol-free progressive dance environment, every Friday night.
- **Dance Freedom** events are held at the First Congregational Church at 11 Garden Street in Cambridge every Wednesday night from 7:30 to 10:45 and every other Saturday night from 8:00 to midnight. They too are an alcohol- and, smoke-free environment.

The following studios offer lessons (everything from Swing to African) and also host participatory dancing events:

- **New Dance Complex**, 536 Mass. Ave., Cambridge, 547-9363
- **Green Street Studio**, 185 Green Street, Cambridge, 864-3191
- **Jamaica Plain Firehouse Art Center**, 659 Centre Street, 524-3816

THEATRE

Boston's theater district officially covers a three to four block area near both the Common and Chinatown, but theaters flourish all over metro

Boston. Often musicals and dramatic plays run in Boston before attempting Broadway. Boston also has a thriving community theater scene in the smaller theaters.

Many of the following theaters and performance centers stage a wide range of events in addition to theater.

- **American Repertory Theatre**, Loeb Drama Center, 60 Brattle Street, Cambridge, 547-8300
- **Berklee Performance Center**, 136 Mass. Ave., Boston, 266-7455
- **Boston Center for the Arts/Cyclorama**, 539 Tremont Street, Boston, 426- 5000
- **Cambridge Multicultural Arts Center**, 41 Second Street, Cambridge, 577- 1400 or 577-1403 for the arts information line
- **Charles Playhouse**, 74 Warrenton Street, Boston, 426-6912
- **Charlestown Working Theatre**, Bunker Hill Street, Charlestown, 242-3285
- **Colonial Theatre**, 106 Boylston Street, Boston, 426-9366
- **Emerson Majestic Theatre**, 219 Tremont Street, Boston, 824-8000
- **Hatch Memorial Shell**, Charles River Esplanade, Boston, 727-9547. (Free concerts and other performances from mid-June to mid-September.)
- **Huntington Theatre Co.**, 264 Huntington Street, Boston, 266-0800
- **John Hancock Hall**, 180 Berkeley Street, Boston, 572-7900
- **Lyric Stage**, 140 Clarendon Street, Boston, 437-7172
- **Sanders Theatre**, Harvard University's Memorial Hall, Cambridge and Quincy Streets, Cambridge, 496-2222
- **Shubert Theatre**, 265 Tremont Street, Boston, 482-9393
- **Strand Theatre**, 543 Columbia Road, Dorchester, 282-8000
- **The Wang Center for the Performing Arts**, 270 Tremont Street, Boston, 482-9393

FREE SUMMER SERIES

There are a number of ways to enjoy free entertainment all summer long:

- **Brookline Recreation Department Concerts**, 730-2070
- **Charles Square Summer Music Series**, 491-5282
- **Cambridgeside Galleria Music Fest**, 621-8666
- **Hatch Memorial Shell Concerts**, 727-9547

- **Concerts at Jamaica Pond**, 725-4505 or 522-7159
- **Newton Arts in the Parks**, 552-7130
- **Summer Stage**, 482-2139 (noon time shows in Downtown Crossing)

COMEDY

Stand-up comedy is alive and well in Boston. One of the national circuit's major venues, Boston sees more than its share of big name comedians. A few places to check out:

- **Nick's Comedy Stop**, 100 Warrenton Street, Boston 482-0930
- **Comedy Connection**, Faneuil Hall Marketplace (middle building, second floor), Boston, 248-9700
- **Comedy Project**, third floor of the Hong Kong restaurant, 1236 Mass. Ave. (Harvard Square), 864-5311
- **Dick Doherty's Comedy Clubs** are at various locations including the Comedy Vault at Remington's, 124 Boylston Street, 267-6626
- **ImprovBoston at the Back Alley Theatre**, 1253 Cambridge Street (Inman Square), Cambridge, 576-1253
- **Guilty Children Improv**, which has no permanent address, 396-2470 for information.

MUSEUMS

ART MUSEUMS

- **DeCordova Museum and Sculpture Park**, Sandy Pond Road, Lincoln, 781-259-8355. The museum is a castle-style building on 35 acres of parkland with an amphitheatre that can seat 1,800.
- **Harvard Semitic Museum**, 6 Divinity Avenue, Cambridge, 495-3123. Features Archeological and artistic exhibits. The museum was founded in 1889.
- **Harvard University Art Museums**, 495-9400. Open seven days a week, 10 a.m. - 5 p.m.; $5 regular admission, free 10 a.m. - Noon Saturdays.
- **Busch-Reisinger Museum**, 32 Quincy Street, Cambridge. German Expressionists.
- **Fogg Art Museum**, 32 Quincy Street, Cambridge. European and American masters in all media.
- **The Arthur M. Sackler Museum**, 485 Broadway, Cambridge. Fine arts and sculpture in the Indian, Asian, Islamic and Ancient traditions.

- **Institute of Contemporary Art**, 955 Boylston Street, Boston, 266-5152 or 266-5151 for the info line. Contemporary art. Painting, sculpture, photography, film, video and live performances. Free admission Thursdays after 5 p.m.
- **Isabella Stewart Gardner Museum**, 280 the Fenway, 566-1401 or 734-1359 for concert information. Mrs. Gardner built this Venetian-style palazzo at the turn of the century to house the results of a lifetime spent collecting European art. A concert series runs from September through June. Free to all students on Wednesdays.
- **Museum of Fine Arts**, 465 Huntington Avenue, Boston, 267-9300. Extensive collections of Asian, Egyptian, Classical Greek and Roman art, and European and American sculpture, textiles, furniture and paintings. Free admission Wednesdays after 4:30 p.m.
- **The Museum of the National Center of Afro-American Artists**, 300 Walnut Avenue, Boston, 442-8614. Call for hours.

MUSEUMS - FREEDOM TRAIL

The **Freedom Trail** is a walking tour of Boston featuring 300 years of history. The **National Park Service** offers guided tours but you can walk the Freedom Trail on your own if you prefer. Start at the Boston Common and follow the painted red line along the sidewalk (sometimes the line is brick). In addition to numerous historical sites and buildings, the Trail takes you past a number of museums that focus on Boston history.

- **Paul Revere House**, 19 North Square (North End), Boston, 523-2338
- **Old State House**, corner of State and Washington, Boston, 720-3290
- **Old South Meeting House**, 310 Washington Street, Boston, 482-6439
- **The U.S.S. Constitution Museum**, Charlestown Navy Yard, 426-1812

MUSEUMS - HISTORICAL

- **Boston Tea Party Ship and Museum**, Congress Street Bridge,

Boston, 338-1773
- **Gibson House Museum**, 137 Beacon Street, Boston, 267-6338
- **Harrison Gray Otis House**, 141 Cambridge Street, Boston, 227-3956
- **Harvard University Museums of Cultural and Natural History**, 24 Oxford Street, Cambridge, 495-3045, including the following collections:
- **The Peabody Museum of Archaeology and Ethnology**
- **The Mineralogical and Geological Museum**
- **The Botanical Museum** houses the **Garden in Glass** (affectionately known as the "Glass Flowers")
- **Museum of Comparative Zoology**
- **The John F. Kennedy Library and Museum**, Columbia Point off Morrisey Boulevard, Dorchester, 929-4500
- **Longfellow National Historic Site**, 105 Brattle Street, Cambridge, 876-4491
- **Museum of Afro-American History**, 46 Joy Street, Boston, 742-1854

MUSEUMS - OTHER

- **The Children's Museum**, 300 Congress Street, Boston, 426-8855
- **The Computer Museum**, 300 Congress Street, Boston, 423-6758
- **Museum of Science**, Science Park, Boston, 723-2500
- **The Sports Museum of New England**, Fleet Center, Boston (library and archive), 787-7678, exhibits in various cities including W.A. Mack Building, 25 Shattuck Street, Lowell, 978-452-6775

ZOOS/AQUARIUMS

- **The Franklin Park Zoo**, Franklin Park, Blue Hill Avenue, Dorchester, 442-4896 or 442-2002
- **New England Aquarium**, Central Wharf off Atlantic Avenue, Boston, 973-5200

MOVIE THEATERS

ART, REVIVAL, NON–MAJOR STUDIO RELEASES

- **Boston Public Library**, Copley Square, 666 Boylston, 536-5400
- **Brattle Theatre**, 40 Brattle Street (Harvard Square), Cambridge 876-6837
- **Brookline Public Library**, 361 Washington Street, Brookline, 730-2368
- **Capital Theatre**, 204 Mass. Ave., East Arlington, 648-4340
- **Coolidge Corner Theatre**, 290 Harvard Street, Brookline, 734-2500
- **Harvard University Film Archive**, 24 Quincy Street, Cambridge, 495-4700
- **Loews Harvard Square**, 10 Church Street, Cambridge, 864-4580
- **Nickelodeon Cinemas**, 34 Cummington Avenue, 424-1500
- **Museum of Fine Arts**, 465 Huntington Street, Boston, 267-9300
- **Newton Free Library**, 330 Homer Street, Newton, 552-7145

LECTURES

Most of Boston's colleges have lecture series. So do many churches, museums and bookstores. Check *The Boston Globe* on Thursdays and the *Boston Herald* on Fridays for listings. You should also check the *Harvard Gazette*. Below is a partial list of lecture series offered in the area.

- **Boston Public Library**, Copley Square, 536-5400, ext. 212
- **Brown Bag Lunch Series at Radcliffe Yard**, 10 Garden Street, Cambridge, 495-8140
- **Cambridge Center for Adult Education**, 56 Brattle Street, Cambridge, 547- 6789
- **Cambridge Public Library Author Series**, 449-Broadway, 349-4040
- **Charles River Conservation Law Headquarters**, 62 Summer Street, Boston, 350-0990
- **Community Church Center of Boston**, 565 Boylston Street, 266-6710
- **The Ethical Society of Boston**, 44 Commonwealth Avenue, 739-9050
- **Ford Hall Forum**, various locations, 337-5800

- **Harvard Events Line**, 495-1718
- **Kennedy Library Forum**, John F. Kennedy Library, Columbia Point, 929-4554
- **MIT Arts Hotline**, 253-2787
- **Museum of Fine Arts**, 465 Huntington Avenue, Boston, 536-3315
- **New Acropolis**, 1152 Beacon Street, Brookline, 277-9422
- **Newton Free Library**, 30 Homer Street, Newton, 552-7145
- **Old South Meeting House**, 310 Washington Street, Boston, 482-6439
- **Pathfinder Books**, 780 Tremont Street, Boston, 247-6772

Radcliffe, Brandeis, Simmons, Northeastern and Boston Universities as well as Hebrew College and Boston College are additional places that offer lecture series. See the **"Education"** chapter for more information.

POETRY READINGS

Boston is full of poets and you'll find poetry readings everywhere. Most of the readings listed here have been around for years but you should call to made sure that times and nights haven't changed.

- **Barnes & Noble** poetry readings, 325 Harvard Street (Coolidge Corner), Brookline, 566-5562, Thursdays
- **The Black Rose** poetry readings, 50 Church Street (Harvard Square), 492-8630, Tuesdays
- **Bookcellar Cafe** poetry readings, 1971 Mass. Ave., Cambridge, 864-9625, Fridays
- **Boston Poetry Slam**, Cantab Lounge, 783 Mass. Ave., Cambridge, 354-2685
- **Kendall Cafe** poetry readings, 233 Cardinal Medeiros Way (Kendall Square), Cambridge, 661-0993, Wednesdays
- **Naked City Coffee Haus**, Old Cambridge Baptist Church, 1150 Mass. Ave. (Harvard Square), Cambridge, 864-9275, every Thursday
- **Redbones Barbeque** poetry readings, 55 Chester Street (Davis Square), Somerville, 628-2200, Sundays
- **Stone Soup Poetry**, T.T. The Bear's, 10 Brookline (Central Square), Cambridge, 227-0845, Mondays

INTERNET ACCESS/ ON-LINE SERVICES

Here's a list of seven national on-line services. Call to find out rates and local access numbers.

- **America Online**, 800-827-6364
- **AT&T**, 800-222-0300
- **CompuServe**, 800-848-8199
- **Microsoft Network**, 800-426-9400
- **Netcom**, 800-638-2661
- **Prodigy**, 800-776-3449
- **Whole Earth Network**, 415-281-6500

DISCOVERING HISTORICAL BOSTON

In colonial days, many sections of what is now Boston's waterfront once served as piers for unloading ships. However, as the city grew, some of the old waterfront was filled in to support the ever-expanding population. Dirt, rubble and buildings torn down in other parts of the city became landfill. Thus quite literally, Boston's historical past provided the foundations for most of what you see today.

Boston's history is that of the United States. It's not difficult to imagine a horse and rider walking the winding cobblestone streets of Boston. Poet John Collins Bossidy paid homage to Boston as "the home of the bean and the cod, where the Lowells talk to Cabots, and the Cabots talk only to God."

A walk along the not-quite three mile **Freedom Trail** is a great way to gain an appreciation of the rich local history, as well as familiarize yourself with the city.

A tour through the **North End** brings you past the **Old North Church**, where the famous signal was sent out to Paul Revere, "One if by land, two if by sea," to issue the warning that the Redcoats were coming. Of course, much of what has been chronicled about Revere's ride is fiction. He was one of several riders on that fateful night, but he was actually captured by the British early in the ride. However, this certainly doesn't diminish the charm of this historic church with its family pews from centuries past.

There's even a chance to witness the famous confrontation with the British in Concord, where the "shot heard round the world" eventually led to the birth of a new nation. Each year enthusiasts re-enact this famous battle on Patriot's Day in April, the same day the **Boston Marathon** is run from Hopkinton to Boston.

Also to be found on the Freedom Trail is the **Granary Burying Ground** which serves as the final resting place for such patriots as **John Hancock, Samuel Adams, Paul Revere** (whose home in the North End is the oldest standing home in Boston), **Mary Goose** (better known as **Mother Goose** to parents and children), and the parents of native son **Benjamin Franklin.** Franklin was born in Boston on January 6, 1706. There are several imitation Ben Franklins working the streets of Boston offering a view of the city from his lifetime, including a Ben Franklin look-alike operating out of the renovated **Old South Meeting House** on Washington at Milk Street.

Another stop on the Freedom Trail is in **Charlestown Navy Yard**, not far from the **Bunker Hill Monument**, where the nation's oldest commissioned war ship, **the USS Constitution,** "Old Ironsides," is anchored. It was at Bunker Hill, then known as Breed's Hill, that Gen. Israel Putnam urged his troops not to fire on the British soldiers until they saw "the whites of their eyes."

George Washington's final visit here in 1789 inspired not only the name of downtown's major thoroughfare but also that of the surrounding streets. After renaming it Washington Street, city fathers added a stipulation to make sure it was different from all other Washington Streets: in Boston, the names of streets crossing Washington are required to be different on one side and the other. For instance, Winter Street on one side of Washington becomes Summer Street on the other side.

The workbench where **Alexander Graham Bell** invented the telephone in Boston in 1876 can be found in the lobby of the headquarters of **New England Bell** on Franklin Street.

Boston was also the site of one of the more bizarre disasters in our nation's history, the great molasses massacre of 1919. On an unseasonably warm January 15 of that year, a molasses tank at the United States Industrial Alcohol Company on the corner of Commercial and Causeway burst. Several tons of gooey molasses oozed forth, gumming up trolley service, bending support pillars on the elevated railway, and crushing, drowning or candying 21 people to death.

Some of the country's oldest eating and drinking establishments are located near Boston's waterfront along the Freedom Trail. **The Union Oyster House**, 227-2750, established in 1826, at 40 Union Street near **Faneuil Hall** is America's oldest restaurant. It is also located near a series of back streets that offer a view of what old Boston looked like before the modern city took hold. You can also visit **The Green Dragon Tavern,** where patriots drank ale and plotted the uprising which became the Revolutionary War at 11 Marshall Street.

The **Warren Tavern** at 2 Pleasant Street in Charlestown, which dates back to 1780, was one of the favorite watering holes of General Washington and Paul Revere.

The rich history of Boston's African-American community is available along the 1.6-mile **Black Heritage Trail,** 742-5415. It's located on the north slope of Beacon Hill, once known as the West End. The attractions include a memorial to a white aristocrat, **Robert Gould Shaw,** who led the all-black 54th Regiment during the Civil War, as well as a stop at the **African Meeting House,** 742-1854.

Other contact numbers: **Greater Boston Convention & Visitors Bureau,** 536-4100; **Cambridge Discovery,** Harvard Square Red Line T Stop, 497-1630. And if you're really interested in Boston's rich and illustrious history, go to a bookstore or library and start reading.

PUBLIC SCHOOLS

Like most big American cities, public schools in Boston run the gamut. In the early 1990s, at least one high school lost its accreditation due to poor quality. But under the leadership of Superintendent Thomas Payzant, who arrived in time for the 1996-97 school year, there were renewed efforts to improve the public schools of Boston.

These include the Boston Arts Academy, the city's first public high school for students showing strong interest in dance, music, theater and visual arts. Then there is also Boston Latin, among the country's elite public high schools, which requires a qualifying entrance exam.

At the elementary school level, full-day kindergartens are available for 5-year-olds, which officials maintain will better prepare students for first grade.

The city's public school system is divided into three zones, North, West and East. Within each zone, parents can take advantage of a choice plan, which allows children within a given zone to choose which school they wish to attend. For more information call the **Boston Public Schools**, 26 Court Street, 635-9265, or parent support services, 635-9660. Also check the Massachusetts Department of Education web site at www.info.doe.mass.edu.

PRIVATE/PAROCHIAL/RELIGIOUS SCHOOLS

Those with the financial resources will be glad to know that there are also a number of well-regarded private schools in the area, including the famous **Phillips Academy** in Andover, about 40 miles north of Boston and **Milton Academy** in Milton, just south of the city. **The Association of Independent Schools in New England** (www.aisne.org) has over

160 member schools throughout the six-state region, beginning with pre-schools. The association can also answer questions for parents leaning toward sending their children to private schools. AISNE is at 100 Grossman Drive, Suite 301, Braintree, MA, 02184, 617-849-3080.

Boston has a large Catholic population, and the **Boston Archdiocese** (www.rcab.org), 781-254-0100, operates an extensive parochial school system. Contact the Catholic Schools Office, 298-6555, to obtain a directory of schools that are attractive to parents who want their children to have a Catholic education.

There are also a number options for students of other religions, from Jewish day schools to Muslim schools. Learn more through the leader of your church, synagogue or religious center.

RESOURCES

Besides the Boston School Department and the Boston School Committee, there are other ways to gain information about the school choices available. One of them is **School Match**, 800-992-5323, a private company that offers ratings of public schools through their web site (www.schoolmatch.com). Also, each Boston public school zone has a **parent center for referral**: West Zone is 635-8040; East Zone is 635-8015; North Zone is 635-9010. Parents of high school age youngsters should call 635-8890.

Perhaps the best way to learn about Boston area schools for your youngster is by talking to friends, family, co-workers, anyone really. The more people you talk to about this important topic, the better informed you'll be and the better choices you'll make.

COLLEGES AND UNIVERSITIES

Metropolitan Boston is home to some of the world's top colleges and universities, which offer everything from an associate degree to the most sought after graduate degrees. Following is a list of some of the better known schools.

BOSTON–CAMBRIDGE

- **Boston University** (www.bu.edu), independent, nonsectarian, coed university located on banks of Charles River in Boston's Back Bay section. BU has 15 schools and colleges, 30,000 students.

Commonwealth Ave. 353-2300.

- **Cambridge College** (www.cambridge.edu), caters mainly to students of color who are in their 30s, offering Masters degrees in education and management and a Bachelor of Arts. 1000 Mass. Ave., 868-1000.
- **Emerson College** (www.emerson.edu), a four-year school of communications and performing arts that numbers among its alumni Tonight Show host Jay Leno. 100 Beacon Street, 824-8500.
- **Emmanuel College** (www.emmanuel.edu), Catholic college that is among the colleges located on the Fenway. 400 The Fenway, 277-9340.
- **Fisher College** (www.fisher.edu), private college offering two-year degrees at two campuses: 118 Beacon Street, 236-8800, and 142 Corporation Road, Hyannis, 508-771-6610.
- **Franklin Institute** (www.franklin-fib.edu), founded with money included as a codicil to the will of Benjamin Franklin, educating men and women in industrial and engineering technology. 41 Berkley Street, 423-4630.
- **Harvard University** (www.harvard.edu), America's oldest, most prestigious university Byerly Hall, 10 Garden Street, 495-1000.
- **Lesley College** (www.lesley.edu), located off Harvard Square, Lesley offers degrees in education and wide range of human services, management and the arts, combining internships with classroom work. 29 Everett Street, 868-9600 or 800-999-1959.
- **Massachusetts College of Art** (www.massart.edu), four-year arts college not far from Museum of Fine Arts. 621 Huntington Avenue, 232-1555.
- **Massachusetts Institute of Technology** (www.mit.edu), one of the premier science universities, draws top graduate and undergraduate students from around the world. Also offers degrees in the arts, humanities and social sciences. 77 Mass. Ave., 258-5515.
- **Northeastern University** (www.neu.edu), located near the Museum of Fine Arts, Northeastern offers a unique internship program in field of study for undergrads as well as grad and law school students. 60 Huntington Avenue, 373-2000.
- **Simmons College** (www.simmons.edu), four-year women's college on the Fenway focusing on liberal arts and sciences and professional education, as well as graduate programs for men and women. 300 The Fenway, 521-2051 or 800-345-8468.
- **Suffolk University** (www.suffolk.edu), located on Beacon Hill in the

heart of the city's business, technology, law, medical and government centers. Suffolk offers undergraduate and graduate degrees in liberal arts and sciences, as well as business and law. Beacon Hill, 573-8000.

- **University of Massachusetts at Boston** (www.umb.edu), Boston branch of the state's university system, located on Boston Harbor next to the John F. Kennedy Presidential Library. 100 Morrissey Boulevard, 287-5000.
- **Urban College**, ABCD (www.bostonabcd.org/urbancol.htm), a two-year college, developed by Action for Boston Community Development, offering the city's inner-city degrees in Human Services Administration, Early Childhood Education, and General Studies. 178 Tremont Street, 357-6000.
- **Wentworth Institute** (www.wit.edu), located on 30-acre campus across from Boston Museum of Fine Arts, offering bachelor's degrees in architecture, design, engineering, technology, and management of technology. Corner of Ruggles Street and Huntington Avenue, 442-9010.
- **Wheelock College** (www.wheelock.edu), another of the colleges located in the Fenway area, offering a four-year undergrad degree and a number of grad programs. 200 The Riverway, 734-5200.

WEST

- **Aquinas College**, Newton, sponsored by Sisters of St. Joseph, offering two-year program of legal studies, business administration and accounting. 15 Walnut Park, 969-4400. There is also a second campus in Milton, 303 Adams Street, 617-696-3100.
- **Babson College**, Wellesley (www.babson.edu), independent school of management education. Babson Park, 781-235-1200.
- **Bentley College**, Waltham, (www.bentley.edu), coed, four-year college offers business and arts and sciences degrees, emphasizing careers in business. 175 Forest Street. 781-891-2000.
- **Boston College**, Chestnut Hill, (www.bc.edu), coed Jesuit-affiliated university located six miles from downtown Boston that is home to 8,500 undergraduates and 4,000 graduate students representing. Office of Undergraduate Admission Devlin Hall 208, 140 Commonwealth Avenue, 800-360-2522 or 552-8000.
- **Brandeis University**, Waltham (www.brandeis.edu), although associated with the Jewish faith, Brandeis offers a first-rate liberal arts

education to students of all religions and ethnic groups. 415 South Street, 736-3500.

- **Lasell College**, Newton (www.lasell.edu), the nation's oldest private two-year college for women until it began granting four-year degrees in 1989. 1844 Commonwealth Avenue, 243-2225
- **Newbury College**, Brookline (www.newbury.edu), college offers degrees ranging from the culinary arts to liberal arts. 1800 Newbury Street, 730-7000.
- **Regis College**, Weston (www.regiscollege.edu), a Catholic, liberal arts and sciences college for women located on a former estate. 235 Wellesley Street, 781-768-7000.
- **Wellesley College**, Wellesley (www.wellesley.edu), elite four-year women's college boasting such alums as Hillary Rodham Clinton. 106 Central Street, 283-1000.

SOUTH

- **Wheaton College**, Norton (www.wheatonma.edu), four-year liberal arts college about 30 miles south of Boston. Wheaton College, 508-285-8200.

NORTH

- **Bradford College**, Haverhill (www.bradford.edu) A coed, four-year liberal arts college located 35 miles north of Boston. 320 South Main Street, 508-372-7161, ext. 5271.

S erving as a volunteer in a new city is beneficial for both you and your new community. Human services and charitable organizations are always under-funded and many organizations rely heavily on volunteer labor. The area's multitude of museums also need help. As a volunteer you will be providing your community with an extremely valuable service—as well as tapping into a social circle with those who share your concerns.

If you'd like to donate your time but you don't know where to start, try one of the following **volunteer workers placement services**:

- **The United Way of Massachusetts Bay**, 245 Summer Street, Boston, 624-8000
- **Chelsea Community Volunteer Center**, 887-2530
- **Oxfam America, Inc.**, 26 West Street, Boston, 482-1211
- **St. Vincent Pallotti Center**, 159 Washington Street, Brighton, 783-3924

You will find volunteer opportunities listed in the newspapers. However, if you're interested in a specific cause consider contacting one of the following organizations directly.

AIDS

- **AIDS Housing Corporation**, 95 Berkeley Street, Boston, 451-2248
- **Haitian Center for Community, Health, Education, Research** (formerly Haitian Community AIDS Outreach Project) , 420 Washington Street, Dorchester, 265-0628
- **Women of Color AIDS Council**, 29 Stanhope Street, Boston, 421-9553

ALCOHOL AND DRUGS

- **Bay Cove Substance Abuse**, 104 Lincoln Street, Boston, 350-6270
- **Habit Management Institute**, 99 Topeka Street, Boston, 442-1499

CHILDREN

- **Boston Children's Services**, 271 Huntington Avenue, Boston, 267-3700
- **Cambridge Family & Child Services**, 929 Mass. Ave., Cambridge, 876-4210
- **Massachusetts Society for the Prevention of Cruelty to Children**, 399 Boylston Street, Boston, 587-1500
- **New England Home for Little Wanderers**, 68 Fargo Street, Boston,783-7070
- **Roxbury Multi-Serv Center, Inc.**, 317 Blue Hill Avenue, Roxbury, 427-4470

DISABLED ASSISTANCE

- **Boston Aid to the Blind**, 1980 Centre Street, West Roxbury, 323-5111
- **Boston Center for Independent Living**, 95 Berkeley Street, Boston, 338-6665
- **Boston Self Help Center**, 18 Williston Road, Brookline, 277-0080
- **Cambridge Law Center for Disability Rights, Inc.**, 2067 Mass. Ave., Cambridge, 492-6789
- **Deaf, Inc.**, 215 Brighton Avenue, Allston, 254-4041
- **Massachusetts Association for the Blind**, 200 Ivy, Brookline, 731-6444

ENVIRONMENT

- **Boston GreenSpace Alliance**, 44 Bromfield Street, Boston, 426-7980
- **Conservation Law Foundation**, 62 Summer Street, Boston, 350-0990
- **Massachusetts Audubon Society**, 208 South Great Road, Lincoln, 781-259-9500
- **Save the Harbor-Save the Bay**, 25 West Street, Boston, 451-2860
- **Sierra Club**, 3 Joy Street, Boston, 227-5339
- **Somerville Environmental & Recycling Volunteers** (SERV), 628-8850

GAY AND LESBIAN

- **Bisexual Community Resource Office**, 29 Stanhope Street, Boston, 424-9595
- **Boston Alliance of Gay and Lesbian Youth**, 800-422-2459
- **Gay & Lesbian Advocates & Defenders**, 294 Washington Street, 426-1350
- **Network for Battered Lesbians and Bisexual Women Office**, 695-0877

HEALTH AND HOSPITALS

- **American Cancer Society**, 654 Beacon Street, Boston, 437-1900
- **American Lung Association of Massachusetts**, 1505 Commonwealth Avenue, Brighton, 787-5864
- **New England Baptist Hospital**, 125 Parker Hill Avenue, 754-5830, ext. 5169
- **Deaconness/Weston Hospital and Medical Center**, 781-647-6302

If there's a hospital in your neighborhood that isn't listed here, give them a call anyway. Most hospitals welcome volunteers.

HOMELESS

- **Cardinal Medieros YMCA Shelter**, 316 Huntington Avenue, Boston, 247- 8956
- **The Mass. Housing and Shelter Alliance**, 5 Park Street, Boston, 367-6447
- **Somerville Homeless Coalition**, 14 Chapel Street, Somerville, 623-6111

HUMAN SERVICES

- **American Red Cross**, 364-0578
- **Bay Cove Human Services, Inc.**, 66 Canal Street, Boston, 371-3000
- **Catholic Charitable Bureau of the Archdiocese of Boston**, 523-5165
- **Combined Jewish Philanthropies of Greater Boston, Inc.**, 330-9500
- **Hospice Federation of Massachusetts**, 1420 Providence Highway,

Norwood, 781-255-7077
- **Urban League of Eastern Massachusetts**, 88 Warren, Roxbury, 442-4519
- **Volunteers of America, Inc.**, 441 Centre Street, Jamaica Plain, 522-8086

LEGAL

- **American Civil Liberties Union**, 99 Chauncey Street, Boston, 482-3170
- **Greater Boston Legal Services**, 197 Friend Street, Boston, 371-1234 or 800-323-3205

MEN'S SERVICES

- **Boston Men's Center**, 9 Willoughby, Brighton, 782-7701

POLITICS

- **Amnesty International**, 58 Day Street, Somerville, 623-0202
- **Bikes Not Bombs**, 59 Amory, Jamaica Plain, 442-0004
- **League of Women Voters**, 133 Portland Street, Boston, 523-2999

SENIOR CITIZENS

- **Mass. Senior Action Council**, 186 Lincoln Street, Suite 901, Boston, 350-6722
- **American Association of Retired Persons**, 723-7600
- **Operation A.B.L.E. of Greater Boston**, 542-4180

WOMEN'S SERVICES

- **Aid to Incarcerated Mothers**, 32 Rutland, Boston, 536-0058
- **Battered Women Support Committee**, 905 Main Street, Waltham, 781-891- 0724
- **Community Services for Women**, 108 Lincoln Street, Boston 482-0747
- **League of Women for Community Service**, 558 Mass. Ave., Boston, 536- 3747
- **National Organization For Women**, 971 Commonwealth Avenue,

Boston, 782-9183
- **Women of Color Coalition for Health**, 3134 Washington Street, Jamaica Plain, 522-7434
- **Women in Community Service**, JFK Federal Building, 565-2180
- **Women's Institute for Housing and Economical Development, Inc.**, 14 Beacon Street, Boston, 367-0520

YOUTH

- **Big Brother/Sister Association**, 285 Martin Luther King Boulevard, Roxbury, 541-9404
- **Jewish Big Brother & Big Sister Association**, 333 Nahanton, Newton Centre, 965-7055
- **Boston Asian Youth Essential Service**, 199 Harrison Avenue, Boston, 482- 4243
- **Boston Street Youth Outreach Program**, 351 Boylston Street, Boston, 247-2005
- **Massachusetts Service Alliance**, 77 Franklin Street, Boston, 542-2544

YOUTH - TUTORING

Many schools welcome volunteers. Here is a partial listing of **Boston area schools** to call:

- Boston, 451-6145
- Brookline, 730-2429
- Cambridge, 349-6794
- Newton, 552-7704
- Somerville, 625-6600 ext. 6175

I f your idea of fun involves physical exercise—your own or watching someone else's—then you'll be excited by all that Boston has to offer. With four professional sports teams, college sports, a wide array of participant sports, and abundant hiking and green space both in Boston itself and in neighboring communities, you should be able to find what you're looking for with little effort.

PROFESSIONAL SPORTS

HOCKEY AND BASKETBALL

The **Fleet Center**, which replaced the venerable Boston Garden is home to both the **Bruins** and the **Celtics**. Professional wrestling, ice skating, and the circus are also staged here.

The Fleet Center has a railroad station and a few eating places and bars. You can get there by taking the Green Line to North Station. Of course you're always welcome to drive if you're willing to tackle the parking nightmare that downtown Boston offers show-goers.

For **information about tickets to Fleet Center events** and box office hours, call 624-1000. You cannot call the Box Office to order tickets — you must purchase them in person. The Box Office accepts Master Card, Visa, American Express, cash and personal checks only if drawn on a Massachusetts bank and written at least 24 hours before the event.

To charge tickets by phone you must call TicketMaster at 931-2000. TicketMaster accepts American Express, Discover, Master Card and Visa and charges a service fee for each ticket. If you go in person to a TicketMaster outlet you must use cash only.

The hockey season for the Boston **Bruins** begins in October and ends in April. The Fleet Center's capacity is 17,565 and the Bruins are popular which means tickets are scarce. Even when the Bruins lose they have a mighty following. You can put your name on a waiting list for season tickets by calling the 227-3206 and listening for the audix system to offer you the option to reach the Bruins administration. They will add your name to the season ticket waiting list over the phone. Ticket prices for the 1997-98 season ranged from $29 to $70. Tickets are available at the Box Office and through TicketMaster (see above). The Bruins web site is www.nhl.com/teams/bos/sitehome.htm.

The Boston **Celtics** share the Fleet Center with the Bruins and their season runs from November through April when the playoffs begin. Seating capacity is 18,600. For Celtics information call 523-6050. Individual tickets are available at the Box Office and through TicketMaster. Ticket prices for the 1997-98 tickets ranged from $10 to $70. (See above for box office and TicketMaster numbers.) After years of being unavailable thanks to the success of the teams led by Larry Bird, Celtic season tickets are available, but may become scarce again due to the arrival of coach Rick Pitino.

Boston Celtics Season Ticket Office
151 Merrimack Street
Boston, MA 021114
The Celtics web site is www.nba.com/celtics.

BASEBALL

The Boston **Red Sox** play at Fenway Park (built in 1912). **Fenway Park,** located right in Kenmore Square (24 Yawkey Way), is small (capacity 34,000), old, and very much loved. Its diminutive size actually makes it a great park for spectators. Baseball season runs from April to October and there are many games. So even though most games sell out, the odds are greater that you will have a chance to see the Red Sox play than the Celtics or the Bruins. Call 267-8661 for schedule and ticket information.

Ticket prices for the 1997 season were $27 for field boxes, $16 for the grandstand and $10 for bleachers. Season tickets are available on a limited basis. You should call 267-8661 before the season starts if you're interested.

You can get to Fenway by taking any Green Line except the E Line Heath to Kenmore Square. Head west one block and you're at the park.

The Red Sox web site is www.redsox.com.

FOOTBALL

The **New England Patriots** play at Foxboro Stadium in Foxboro, Massachusetts, a large stadium (capacity 61,000) approximately 45 minutes south of Boston. Call 800-543-1776 for Patriots ticket information. Their season runs from September to January with a few pre-season games in August. The NFL releases the schedule in early May.

Ticket prices generally range from $26 to $60. Public transportation from South Station to the games is available but the stadium is set up for parking in a way that neither Fenway Park or the Garden could possibly be (due to their locations). If you're interested in taking public transportation, call 508-543-0350 for event specific information.

The Patriots' web site is www.patriots.com.

SOCCER

The **New England Revolution**, a Major League Soccer team, also calls Foxboro Stadium its home. The season runs from April to September. Seating capacity is reduced to 22,000 from the football season.

Season tickets are available. Individual seats range from $10 to $25. Call 508-543-0350. The team's web address is www.mlsnet.com/inside/revolution.

COLLEGE SPORTS

If professional sports are just too expensive or perhaps too impersonal for your tastes, attending a game at one of the area's colleges or universities may be more your style. Harvard University alone has 40 varsity teams.

However, tickets for some of the annual college events can be as hard to get as tickets to professional games. As a matter of fact, tickets for the final match of the **Bean Pot** (a series of hockey matches between Boston's universities played every February) are usually impossible to get. The annual **Harvard vs. Yale football game** is another big attraction.

Here are some places for you to start:

- **Boston College** football, hockey and basketball always offer exciting games. For information call 552-3000.
- **Harvard University** football tickets are still relatively inexpensive.

For information call 495-2211
- **UMass/Boston** basketball, played at Clark Athletic Center at the Columbia Point campus, is probably the best deal in town. Call 287-7800 for information.

You can also check out sporting events at **Northeastern University**, 373-4700, and **Tufts University**, 628-5000.

RACING

- Horseracing at **Foxboro**, 508-543-3800
- Horseracing at **Suffolk**, 567-3900
- Greyhound racing at **Wonderland**, 284-1300

OTHER SPECTATOR SPORTS EVENTS

The world-famous **Boston Marathon** is run from Hopkinton to Copley Square on Patriot's Day every year. Patriot's Day is a holiday only for the Commonwealth of Massachusetts which commemorates the "shot heard round the world" on Lexington Green on April 19, 1775. To the rest of the world, Patriot's Day is simply the third Monday in April.

The **Boston Athletic Association**, 236-1652, has run the Marathon since its beginning in 1897. To join in the fun all you have to do is bring a blanket and a portable radio and locate a suitable spot along the route. The Marathon is cause for a number of other events staged around the big day: the Sports and Fitness Expo, the Carbo-Loading Party the night before, and the Awards Ceremony which is usually over before the majority of participants even finish the race.

In June of each year you can watch the annual **John F. Kennedy Regatta** in Boston Harbor. For information call 847-1800.

Don't miss the **Head of the Charles Regatta**, usually held during the third weekend in October. College crews from all over the nation converge on Cambridge/Boston to compete in this event which runs from the Boston University Boathouse to the Christian Herter Center in Allston. Find a spot along the Charles and enjoy the show. Call 864-8415 for information.

PARTICIPANT SPORTS

If you're interested in **crewing** a boat, start with Community Rowing at Daly Rink on the Charles in Brighton, 782-9091. Their info line is: 455-1992 The facility is open from April through October.

There are a number of intramural **hockey** leagues and teams around but it can be hard to break in as a newcomer. If you're interested in playing hockey with a team there are a number of ways to go about it. Area bars sponsor teams so you could visit local pubs in your neighborhood and ask around. Get to know families who have lived in the area for more than one generation. Visit the ice rinks to find out who has rented space and when, then talk to the organizers when they show up for their ice time. Check the sports pages for ads. Sometimes organizations will advertise for players in the *Globe*.

To join a team in a **softball** league, call the recreation department of your town. Some municipalities are getting strict about requiring proof of residence to play on a town league. Once again, ask around in neighborhood bars or sporting goods stores to find out who sponsors teams.

INDIVIDUAL SPORTS

The Metropolitan District Commission (MDC) is the organization that serves the greater Boston area when it comes to recreation and individual sports. The MDC has several district offices. If you need additional information on any event or facility in your neighborhood, call the MDC office that handles your area:

- **Charles District**, 727-4708. Covers Boston, Belmont, Brighton, Cambridge, Charlestown, the North End, Somerville, Waltham, Watertown
- **Harbor and Neponset Districts**, 727-6034. Covers Cleveland Circle, Jamaica Plain, West Roxbury

BICYCLING

There are a number of bicycle paths in and around Boston as well as bicycling organizations that organize bike trips around New England.

The Charles River has an 18-mile multi-use paved path between

Science Park and Watertown Square known officially as the **Dr. Paul Dudley White Charles River Bike Path** but is usually referred to as the Charles River Bike Path. This path is probably the most highly used recreation space in the city. It's usually filled with runners, bicyclists, in-line skaters and people just out for a stroll. The path is separate from the city but connects at several points by ramped pedestrian bridges so there's plenty of access.

A mini-trail runs from Jamaica Pond through Olmstead Park and along the Riverway.

The **Stony Brook Reservation Bike Path** runs along Turtle Pond Parkway, starting at Hyde Park's River Street and ending at Washington Street in West Roxbury. The trail is almost four miles long.

The **Minute Man Bicycle Trail** is a 12-mile path from Alewife Train Station to Bedford, MA. There are lots of places along the way to catch the trail. Many in-line skaters also use this trail.

The **Mystic River Reservation Bike Path** runs for approximately three and a half miles from the Wellington Bridge in Everett to the Wellington ridge in Somerville.

Wompatuck State Park has 12 miles of bike trails. The park is in Hingham off Route 228. There is a bicycle trail system in Lincoln and Concord. Another option is just to head west and bike along the tree-lined back roads.

The **Harborwalk** is also a seaside path running from the North end to the South end.

If you're interested in bicycling with a group you could start with:
- **American Youth Hostels**, 1020 Commonwealth Ave., 731-5430
- **Bicycle Coalition of Massachusetts**, 491-7433 (also call them for maps)

BOATING

With the Harbor, the Mystic River and the Charles River at their disposal, metro Boston inhabitants spend a lot of time on or near the water. The Charles River is over 80 miles long and many of the communities and neighborhoods mentioned in this guide are located along it. The Charles is Boston's backyard waterway, accessible to the majority of its inhabitants. If you run, walk, bike, skate or go to concerts you will be hard pressed not to spend some time along the Charles. And if you sail or row you absolutely won't be able to avoid it.

Boats of any type (except inflatables), canoes, kayaks and rowboats are allowed both on the Charles and in the inner harbor. The MDC and the City of Boston run boating and sailing programs and lessons for both children and adults.

The **Community Boating School**, which offers sailing lessons and organizes boating programs, has handled sailing for the MDC since 1950. The Boathouse itself was built in 1940 with money from Helen Osborn Storrow. It's located at 21 Embankment Road on the Charles River Esplanade between the Longfellow Bridge and the Hatch Shell. Call 523-7406 for details.

The MDC also runs a number of **small boat launches** in Boston, Medford and Nahant. Call the Harbor Master, 727-0537 for details and locations.

You should also try some of the following boathouses and centers:

- **Boston Harbor Sailing Club**, 72 East India Row, Boston, 523-2619
- **Boston Sailing Center**, 54 Lewis Wharf, Boston, 227-4198. Lessons, membership, racing programs. Open year round.
- **Community Rowing**, Daly Rink, Nonanutum Road, Brighton, 782-9091
- **Charles River Canoe and Kayak Center**, 2401 Commonwealth Avenue, Newton, 965-5110, offers guided trips and lessons and canoe, kayak and scull rentals.
- **Jamaica Pond Boathouse**, located on the Jamaicaway in Jamaica Plain, 522-6258. Sailing lessons, rowboat and sail boat rentals available from June to September.

HIKING, ROCK CLIMBING AND MOUNTAINEERING

Also see the chapter on **Green Space** below.
The MDC maintains hiking trails at six area reservations. This means you can commune with the trees without traveling for hours: most of these reservations offer some wilderness within 15 miles (or less!) of Boston.

- **Blue Hills Reservation**, Milton and Canton
- **Beaverbrook Reservation**, Belmont
- **Breakheart Reservation**, Saugus
- **Hemlock Gorge**, Newton Upper Falls
- **Middlesex Fells Reservation**, runs through Medford, Malden,

Melrose, Stoneham, Winchester
• **Belle Isle Marsh Reservation**, East Boston

You should also check into the trails through **Walden Woods** in Concord and through the **Lincoln Woods Reservation** which connects with Walden Woods. Expect Lincoln and Walden Woods to be well-populated at all times of the year. The reservations will offer you more of a wilderness experience but they are well used, too.

If you are interested in **rock climbing**, you should try the Quincy Quarries near the Blue Hills Reservation and Menotomy Rocks Park in Arlington. You can keep your rock climbing skills honed year-round by joining the **Boston Rock Gym**, an indoor facility with climbing walls, located at 78 Olympia in Woburn. Call 935-7325 for information.

If you are interested in the outdoors and learning new outdoor skills you should know about two organizations: the Appalachian Mountain Club and Mountain Lynx Outdoor Adventure School.

Located at 5 Joy Street in Boston, 523-0636, the **Appalachian Mountain Club** conducts hiking and skiing tours and trips and maintains a cabin system in the White Mountains which members can use. Joining this club would be a good way to tap into the hiking scene.

Mountain Lynx Outdoor Adventure School, 508-840-6464, is located in Leominster, not Boston, but the instructors conduct classes on climbing, hiking, spelunking, canoeing, camping, team building and rope skills right in the Boston area. Mountain Lynx also offers classes in winter camping and ice climbing in the White Mountains as well as custom designed programs and courses for schools and other groups.

GOLF

The Boston area features a number of public 18-hole golf courses with a 36-hole course at the Blue Hills Reservation. Most courses are open from dawn to dusk and require reservations on weekends and holidays. It's always best to call ahead.

• **Braintree Municipal**, 101 Jefferson Street, Braintree, 843-9781
• **Fresh Pond**, 691 Huron Avenue, Cambridge, 349-6282 (9 holes)
• **George Wright**, 420 West Street, Hyde Park, 361-8313
• **Green Hill Park**, Marsh Avenue, Worcester, 508-852-0913
• **Leo J. Martin Memorial**, 190 Park Road, Weston, 781-894-4903

- **Newton Commonwealth**, Kenrick Street, Newton, 630-1971
- **Ponkapoag**, Blue Hills Reservation, Canton, 781-828-4242
- **William J. Divine**, Blue Hill Avenue, 1 Jewish War Veterans Drive, Dorchester, 265-4084

If you're interested in joining a private club, check the Yellow Pages under Golf Courses-Private.

HORSEBACK RIDING

A number of area stables offer both lessons and rentals. Horseback riding is allowed on Blue Hills Reservation trails. Call the Reservation for information, 698-1802.

- **Canton Equestrian Center**, 151 Randolph, Canton, 781-821-5527
- **Lazy S Ranch**, 300 Randolph, Canton, 781-828-1681
- **Revere/Saugus Riding Academy**, 122 Morris, N. Revere, 781-322-7788

ICE SKATING

The MDC maintains a number of ice rinks in the area. A partial listing is offered:

- **Daly Rink**, Newton, 527-1741
- **Steriti Memorial Rink**, Boston, 523-9327
- **Reilly Memorial Rink**, Brighton, 727-6034 (has rentals)
- **Daly Memorial Outdoor Rink**, Brighton, 727-4708 (has rentals)
- **Simoni Memorial Rink**, Cambridge, 354-9523
- **Emmons-Horrigan-O'Neill Memorial Rink**, Charlestown, 242-9728
- **Bajko Memorial Rink**, Hyde Park, 727-6034
- **LoConte Memorial Rink**, Medford, 781-395-9594
- **Flynn Memorial Rink**, Medford, 781-395-8492
- **Shea Memorial Rink**, Quincy, 472-9325
- **Veterans Memorial Rink**, Somerville, 727-4708
- **Veterans Memorial Rink**, Waltham, 781-727-4708
- **Bryan Memorial Rink**, West Roxbury, 727-6034
  Larz Andersen Park in Brookline also offers an outdoor rink during

winter months. Another truly Boston experience is to skate on the duck pond in the **Boston Public Garden.**

In addition to the MDC rinks listed above, the Town of Watertown runs a private rink: **Watertown Skating Arena**, 1 Paramount Place, Watertown, 972-6468 (rentals available).

IN–LINE SKATING

In-line skating is popular in Boston. If you're not daring enough to skate in the streets there are still many places to use your blades. For fun with gravity (i.e. hills) try the Arnold Arboretum. For distance try the Charles River Bicycle Trail and the Minute Man Bicycle Trail.

Some community and adult-education schools offer lessons and classes. **Beacon Hill Skate In-Line Skate School**, 135 Charles Street South, 482-7400 and **Boston In-Line Skate School**, 51 Philips, Boston, 248-3838 both offer lessons.

For rentals try:

- **Beacon Hill Skate Shop**, 135 Charles Street South, Boston, 482-7400
- **Eric Flaim's Motion Sports**, 349 Newbury, Boston, 247-3284
- **Green Street Skate Shop**, 165 Green, Jamaica Plain, 524-9822
- **Laughing Alley Bike and Skate**, 51 Harvard Avenue, Allston, 783-5832

RACQUET SPORTS – TENNIS AND SQUASH

A number of area health clubs offer racquetball, squash, handball and tennis courts. However, the MDC does maintain public tennis courts where you can play for free. Call the MDC office that covers your neighborhood for information (see the beginning of Individual Sports above). The unlit courts are open until dusk. The lighted courts are open until 11:00 p.m.

Hyde Park
Charles F. Weider Playground, Dale Street, lighted
Francis D. Martini Music Shell, Truman Parkway
John H. Dooley Memorial Playground, Reservation Pond
Medford

Hormel Stadium, four lighted

North End
North End Park, Commercial Street

Quincy
Willard Street at Shea Rink

Somerville
George Dilboy Field, Alewife Brook Parkway
Saxton J. Foss Park, McGrath Highway at Broadway

West End
Charlesbank Park, Charles Street, lighted
Southwest Corridor Park, along the Orange Line, lighted

Boston Common and the **Esplanade** also have tennis courts. Check the Yellow Pages for a list of private tennis courts.

Squash is also popular in Boston. Many clubs have squash courts and so do the colleges. Probably the most famous place for squash is the **Harvard Club**, 374 Commonwealth Ave., Boston 536-1260, a private club. The **Allston-Brighton Squash & Fitness Club**, 15 Gorham, Allston, 731-4177, is a public squash court.
Check the Yellow Pages for a list of private squash courts.

RUNNING

Whether you're running for the workout or because you'd like to race, Boston is the place for you. There are many beautiful areas to run through and bodies of water to run around and alongside. And if you'd like to run competitively, keep in mind some of the area's annual races.

Most of the races listed below are open to amateurs and you'll find notice of them on flyers around town. The list includes the general time period in which they are run. If you don't see or hear anything about a race that you might be interested in you could contact the **Boston Athletic Association**, 236-1652 or go to **Bill Rogers Running Center** at Faneuil Hall Marketplace, 723-5612 to get more information.

• **Run For Peace**, Cambridge, April

- **Boston Milk Run**, Boston, April
- **Boston Marathon**, Hopkinton to Boston, Patriot's Day, April. Call the Boston Athletic Association for qualifying times, eligibility and how to register for this world-famous event, 236-1652
- **Charles River Run**, Boston, May
- **Women on the Run**, Cambridge, May
- **Freedom Trail Race**, Boston/Cambridge, October
- **Turkey Trot**, Boston, Thanksgiving Day

SKIING – CROSS COUNTRY

If winter brings enough snow you can actually ski in the city, especially along the **Emerald Necklace** (see Green Space, below). Arnold Arboretum offers both flat stretches and hills.

Cross country skiing is permitted in all MDC reservations. Check the list in Hiking, above. In addition, try **Great Brook Farm State Park** in Carlisle, 508-369-6312, the **Lincoln Reservation, Lincoln Guide Service**, 259-1111, and the **Weston Ski Touring Center**.

The Weston Ski Touring Center, located at MetroParks Martin Golf Course, makes snow, rents skis and gives lessons. Call 891-6575.

In your search for cross country ski territory please be respectful. Those cemeteries are certainly tempting but skiing in them is not allowed.

SKIING – DOWNHILL

If you want to practice locally and you don't care about the size of the hill, head to Blue Hills Reservation where you'll find the **Blue Hills Ski Area**. It sports three lit slopes, snow making, a ski school and a double chair lift.

If you're looking for mountains, they're not very far away. Ski areas in Western Mass, New Hampshire, Vermont or Maine are available within two to four hours drive of Boston.

SWIMMING – BEACHES

The MDC maintains 16 miles of regularly cleaned ocean beaches and most of them are accessible by public transportation. Beaches are open from the end of June to Labor Day. Call 727-5114, ext. 550 for details.

- **Constitution Beach**, East Boston, take the Blue Line to Orient Heights.
- **Lovells Island**, Boston Harbor, take the Blue Line to Aquarium. Take the ferry to Georges Island and catch a free water taxi to Lovells Island.
- **Malibu Beach**, Dorchester, take the Red Line to Savin Hill.
- **Savin Hill Beach**, Dorchester, take the Red Line to Savin Hill.
- **Tenean Beach**, Dorchester, take the Red Line to Fields Corner. Then take the Neponset bus to Pope's Hill Street.
- **Carson Beach, Castle Island Beach, City Point Beach, Pleasure Bay Beach and M Street Beach**, South Boston, take the Red Line to Broadway. Take the City Point bus to the end of the line.

Other MDC beaches within 10 miles of Boston are:
- **King's Beach** (Lynn)
- **Lynn Beach**
- **Nahant Beach**
- **Revere Beach**
- **Winthrop Beach**
- **Nantasket Beach** (Hull)
- **Wollaston Beach** (Quincy)

As a general rule, don't swim in the Charles.

SWIMMING – POOLS

The MDC also maintains a number of swimming pools open from the end of June to Labor Day. A partial list of MDC Pools follows. Call the MDC office that covers your neighborhood for rates and hours of operation.

- **Brighton/Allston Pool**, Brighton
- **Connors Memorial Pool**, Waltham
- **Dealtry Memorial Pool**, Watertown
- **Dilboy Field Pool**, Somerville
- **Latta Brothers Memorial Pool**, Somerville
- **Lee Memorial Pool**, Boston
- **McCrehan Memorial Pool**, Cambridge
- **Phelan Memorial Pool**, West Roxbury
- **Reilly Memorial Pool**, Brighton
- **Veterans Memorial Pool**, Cambridge

The city of Boston operates a number of pools year round and two pools seasonally. City of Boston pools are maintained through the Community Center Program. For general information call 635-4920. Call for rates and hours of operation. A partial list follows:

- **Blackstone Community Center**, 50 West Brookline, Boston, 635-5162
- **Charlestown Community Center**, 255 Medford, Charlestown, 635-5169
- **Clougherty Pool**, Bunker Hill, Charlestown, 635-5173 - seasonal
- **Condon Community Center**, 200 D Street, South Boston, 635-5100
- **Flaherty Pool**, 160 Florence, Roslindale, 635-5181
- **Mirabella Pool**, Commercial, Boston, 635-5235 - seasonal
- **Quincy Community Center**, 885 Washington Street, Boston, 635-5129
- **West Roxbury Community Center**, 1205 VFW Parkway, West Roxbury, 635-5189

For pools in neighboring communities call your town or city hall or check with your town or city recreation department.

HEALTH CLUBS

There are hundreds of health clubs in the metro Boston area. No doubt you will choose one based on convenience and services. Here are a few to start your search:

- **Beacon Hill Athletic Club**, 3 Hancock Street, Boston, 367-2422
- **Boston Fitness for Women**, 27 School Street, Boston, 523-3098
- **Wellbridge Health and Fitness Center**, 695 Atlantic Avenue, Boston, 439- 9600; 1079 Commonwealth Avenue, Boston, 254-1711
- **Boston Sports Club**, 561 Boylston Street, Boston, 536-1247
- **Cambridge Racquet and Fitness Club**, 215 First Street, Cambridge, 491-8989
- **Fitcorp – Longwood Medical Area**, 350 Longwood Avenue, Boston, 732-7111
- **Fitcorp – Waltham Route 128**, 1601 Trapelo Road (at Route 128), 890-8422

- **The Flatley Fitness Center**, 529 Main Street, Charlestown, 242-6103
- **Healthworks Fitness Center for Women**, 920 Commonwealth Avenue, Brookline, 731-3030
- **Planet Fitness Centers**, 200 Boston Avenue, Medford, 781-393-2500
- **The Newton Marriott Health Club**, 2345 Commonwealth Avenue, Newton, 969-1000, ext. 7806
- **Fitcorp,** One Enterprise Drive, North Quincy, 472-8746
- **The No Frills Aerobic Factory**, 624 Somerville Avenue, Somerville, 625-2700
- **South End Fitness Center**, 35 Northampton, Boston, 534-5822
- **The Boston Sports Club**, 15 Gorham Street, Allston, 731-4177
- **The WellBridge Center**, 135 Wells Avenue, Newton, 244-7882
- **Weston Racquet Club,** 132 West Street, Waltham, 890-4285

For one of the best fitness deals in town, the **YMCA** is always an option.

- Allston/Brighton, 470 Washington Street, 782-3535
- Central Branch, 316 Huntington Street, 536-7800
- Dorchester, 776 Washington Street, 436-7750
- Hyde Park, 1137 River Street, 361-2300
- Roxbury, 285 Martin Luther King Blvd, 427-5300
- South Cove/Chinatown, 56 Tyler Street, 426-2237
- Waltham, 725 Lexington Street, 781-894-5295
- West Roxbury/Roslindale, 15 Bellevue Street, 323-3200
- Woburn, 137 Lexington Street, 781-935-3270

Boston is truly blessed with an abundance of green space. The city and surrounding communities have parks, waterways, reservoirs with park land around them, reservation land and arboretums. Even the cemeteries are spectacular — Mt. Auburn Cemetery is a bird-watcher's paradise, a semi-arboretum with tags marking species on most of the trees.

The heart of Boston is really **Boston Common**, established in 1634 by the people for the people. The Common was functional, open pasture which ran down to the salt marshes at the Charles River. During the Commons' early days, the major recreational activity was "promenading." The colonial militia trained for the Revolutionary War here. The Redcoats occupied the Common for eight years beginning in 1768. Anti-slavery meetings were held here before and during the Civil War.

Today, the Common has shrunk, its original four hills have been leveled, cattle graze only once a year during the Cows on the Common event, and the subway runs underneath it, but it is still Boston's most popular outdoor space for "public assembly and free speech." And the Freedom Trail begins here in the oldest park in the United States. The Common's location, in the heart of downtown, makes it a neighborhood park for those who live on Beacon Hill, Back Bay and Chinatown. The Common is separated from Back Bay by **Boston Public Garden**.

Boston Public Garden, or the Gardens for short, was established in 1837. It was created as a public botanical garden, the first in the nation. The Gardens is a Victorian style park that uses greenhouse-grown annuals assuring that blooms are seen at their peak. You should stop in for a ride on one of the Swan Boats (call 522-1966 for information) and look for the "Make Way For Ducklings" statue. FYI: bicycling and in-line skating are not permitted in the Gardens.

Commonwealth Avenue Mall is a formal avenue with 35 acres of green space that runs the length of Back Bay. Until the mid-1800s Back

Bay really was a bay — or, rather, tidal flats — of the Charles. Starting in 1857, gravel from quarries in west Needham was shipped in trains and dumped into the tidal flats. Nearly 30 years later the Back Bay landfill project was completed. It was an amazing feat. Back Bay's unique architectural structure — French influenced Victorian — still survives. Commonwealth Avenue Mall was created in the French Victorian style by Arthur Gilman during the landfill project. Today, the mall is lined with sweetgum, green ash, maple, linden, zilkova, Japanese pagoda and elm trees.

Commonwealth Avenue Mall links the Public Garden to the **Back Bay Fens** which continues the park system known as the Emerald Necklace. The Common, the Gardens, and Commonwealth Avenue Mall are the only parks in the Necklace that Frederick Law Olmstead didn't create for Boston during the late 1800s. Olmstead is also well known for his design of Central Park in New York City.

Olmstead created the **Back Bay Fens** park in response to problems that arose from damming the Charles (necessary in order to make Back Bay). To be quite blunt, it stank. He flushed out the waterways and tried to create a semblance of the original tidal marsh ecosystem. It didn't work because damming the Charles ultimately changed the water from brackish to fresh. The greenery is different since Olmstead's original vision but the Fens are still much used and appreciated.

The Riverway is the result of Olmstead re-routing the Muddy River as a public health improvement that went along with flushing out the fens. With its steep, tree-filled banks, this park gives you the sense that you really are in the woods. The carriage roads and bridle paths are now used as bike paths.

Olmstead didn't have to use such drastic measures to create the park that still carries his name, **Olmstead Park**. This area is sort of an informal boundary between Boston and Brookline. His original vision was to have the park serve as an educational display with small pools used as natural history exhibits. Today however, the pools are filled in. Olmstead Park features Wards Pond and Leverett Pond, peaceful retreats from the busy medical area nearby, and Daisy Field, a community softball diamond.

Jamaica Pond, the largest body of water in Boston, is a kettlehole left behind by the Ice Age. Jamaica Plain was once a summer retreat for Boston's wealthiest citizens and Jamaica Pond was the site of their summer homes. The city bought the land, removed the houses and an ice-cutting industry, and Olmstead restored it to what he called "a natural sheet of water with quiet graceful shores. . ." Today Jamaica Pond is a living, daily part of Jamaica Plain's community life with free concerts, children's programs and other community events at the boathouse. Runners, skaters, dogwalkers, and promenaders all share the pond.

A little farther south and west of Jamaica Pond you will find **Arnold Arboretum**, 265 acres of trees in the midst of a busy city. For this jewel in the Emerald Necklace, Olmstead collaborated with Charles Sprague Sargent, a scientist who collected thousands of specimens. Olmstead planned the road system and the planting system. The Arboretum features a remarkable collection of maples, crabapples, lilacs and rhododendrons and has over 15,000 vines, trees and shrubs documented and identified. Harvard University has leased the Arboretum from the city for 1,000 years in a unique agreement: the University maintains the greenery and the city maintains the roads and walls.

Franklin Park and Zoo lies south and slightly east of the Arboretum. Franklin Park consists of 527 acres which makes it the largest park in the Necklace. Olmstead created it as a "country park." It has scenery to soothe the savage city soul, a woodland preserve, a zoo, a golf course, and the Playstead for sports events and active recreation. Franklin Park was named after Ben Franklin when the Park Commissioners thought they could get money from the Franklin trust to build the park. They didn't get the cash but the name stuck. For information about the Zoo, call 442-2002.

The Emerald Necklace is by no means the only green space available to you in the Boston area. The **Charles River** area is accessible to many communities. Beacon Hill/West End, Back Bay, Allston/Brighton, Cambridge, Watertown, Newton and Waltham all border the Charles. In addition to the previously mentioned bike trail there are a number of playgrounds, outdoor theaters, boathouses and ice rinks along the Charles. This area is called the **Esplanade** and is where you'll find the Hatch Memorial Shell as well.

Waterfront Park (also known as Christopher Columbus Park) is located right at the edge of Boston Harbor. It sports a playground built with a nautical theme and offers an incredible view of the ocean.

Brookline has a number of beautiful parks and green spaces including **Larz Anderson Park**, the **Brookline Reservoir** and a smaller version of Newton's **Hammond Pond Park** by the same name.

Arlington enjoys **Spy Pond, Menotomy Rocks Park**, and the lakes bordering Medford: **Upper Mystic Lake** and **Lower Mystic Lake**. **Little Pond, Clay Pit Pond** and the **Cambridge Reservoir** are all located in Belmont. The **Mt. Auburn Cemetery**, an arboretum in its own right, is located between Watertown and Cambridge.

Cambridge has **Fresh Pond**. Charlestown has its **Navy Yard** and **Bunker Hill Square**. West Roxbury and Roslindale inhabitants enjoy the **Stony Brook Reservation**. Newton has a number of country clubs, **Cold Spring Park, Crystal Lake** and the **Hammond Pond Reservation**. Waltham enjoys **Prospect Hill Park** and a large amount of private green space is owned by area schools and institutions. There's also another **Cambridge Reservoir** in Waltham.

If you're willing to travel a little, the area's reservations (nature preserves) are available to you. **Middlesex Fells Reservation** and **Blue Hills Reservation** have miles and miles of trails for hiking and mountain biking. Both reservations have carriage paths built by CCC labor. Bikes are not allowed on the foot trails which are designed to give you a challenging climb if you want it. It's possible to complete simple loops or to hike from end to end along the Sky Line Trails. Blue Hills Reservation features a wheel-chair accessible boardwalk through a bog. Following is a list of MDC area reservations:

- **Blue Hills Reservation**, Milton and Canton
- **Beaverbrook Reservation**, Belmont
- **Breakheart Reservation**, Saugus
- **Hemlock Gorge**, Newton Upper Falls
- **Middlesex Fells Reservation**, runs through Medford, Malden, Melrose Stoneham, Winchester
- **Belle Isle Marsh Reservation**, East Boston

Walden Pond and **Walden Woods** in Concord are only 20 minutes away. You can learn about Henry David Thoreau, visit a re-creation of his cabin, visit its original site, go on a walking tour with the Thoreau Society or just do your own thing — hike, swim, skate or ski (depending on the season). In addition to its connection with Thoreau, Walden Pond is also special because its origin as a glacial kettle means it has excellent drainage. The water remains clean and clear throughout the summer.

Some of Boston's most underutilized natural resources are the **Harbor Islands**. There are fishing and boat piers, guided walks, historic forts and ruins, and picnic areas on most of them. Bring fresh water and food because the only island that offers refreshments is George's. To get to the islands, take a ferry ride from Boston (you can get them at Long Wharf) or Hingham to George's Island. From George's you can take a free water taxi to Bumpkin, Gallops, Grape, Lovells or Peddocks. Call the following agencies for information, camping permits and reservations.

The Massachusetts Department of Environmental Management, 740-1605, manages Bumpkin, Calf, Gallops, Grape and Great Brewster Islands.

The MDC, 727-5290, manages Lovells, Peddocks and George's Island.

The Thompson Island Outward Bound Education Center, 328-3900 owns Thompson Island. This island is open to the public on a limited basis.

Traveling in Boston can be very confusing, especially with the multi-billion dollar reconstruction project known as the "Big Dig" that will convert the Central Artery (Interstate 93) through the city's Financial District along Boston Harbor from an elevated to an underground roadway. The project is scheduled to be completed in the early part of the new century. Pay close attention to the ever-changing signs for directions.

You may also find yourself driving for blocks without knowing what street you're on because although the cross streets are marked, the street that you're on is not. The expressways and major highways can save you some time depending on the time of day. However, during rush hours you'll more than likely return to the streets, no matter how narrow or crooked, looking for ways to avoid being caught in gridlock on the major arteries.

One thing you should be aware of is that *all the stereotypes about Boston drivers are true*. Boston drivers are assertive and expressive. You may have to "go native" to get where you're going.

For the uninitiated, the most intimidating New England traffic institution is known as the "rotary" or "roundabout." These are often used instead of traffic lights especially when more than two streets intersect. Traffic already in the circle has the legal right of way but the real rule of the road is a combination of "no guts no glory" and "go with the flow." Get in there and circle around to your exit. Remember: s/he who hesitates is lost. Once you get the hang of it you'll have to agree that it is an efficient way to move cars around.

Some of the major highways and byways are as follows.

- **I93** links up with **Route 3** in Quincy heading north (Route 3 south goes to Cape Cod). These combined routes form the Central Artery through downtown Boston. Route 3 breaks off before the Charles, takes a jag south, crossing to Cambridge over the Longfellow Bridge, then heads west where it is also known as Memorial Drive. I93 links up with Route 1 and they cross over the Charles River and split up in Charlestown: Route 1 heads north east up the coast and I93 heads west.

- **Route 1** is one of those disappearing/reappearing streets this area is famous for. It comes up through the south through Dedham and West Roxbury. It becomes the Arborway/Jamaicaway/Riverway /Fenway and then disappears. It reappears combined with I93 as described above.
- **Route 2** is also Commonwealth Ave. until it crosses the Charles at the Boston University Bridge where it joins Route 3 and Memorial Drive. Once Memorial Drive veers into the Fresh Pond Parkway (heading west) Route 3 turns into Route 2A briefly and Route 2 heads west in a northerly fashion.
- **I90** is the Massachusetts Turnpike, known as the Pike. It begins at the Central Artery and heads west through Boston. I95 and Route 128 are combined in a semi-circular loop that skirts Boston and the suburbs along the western edge heading north. Please note that it is a toll road.
- **Route 9** is also Huntington Avenue in Boston and Boylston Street in Brookline and Newton. Route 9 heads west and south through Boston, Brookline and Newton where it links with 128/95.
- **The Fenway** begins where Boylston veers around the Fens. The Fenway heads south along the Fens and the Emerald Necklace. It becomes the Riverway which becomes the Jamaica Way which becomes the Arborway. The Arborway is also Route 203.

Are you confused yet? Don't despair. Learning your way around metro Boston by car is a challenge that can be mastered only by trial and error. It's also quite fulfilling once you've discovered how to get across town during rush hour without getting trapped in traffic. Ex-Bostonians report boredom with cities that are laid out on a grid. After all, where's the challenge if the street doesn't double back on itself and its name doesn't change two or three times along the way?

If you'd like to start or join a carpool call **Caravan for Commuters, Inc.**, a private non-profit organization. Call 227-7665 or 888-426-6688. Its web site is www.commute.com.

PUBLIC TRANSPORTATION WITH THE MBTA (THE "T")

The Massachusetts Bay Transit Authority (MBTA) is Boston's public trans-portation system. Often it is just called the "T" because its symbol is the capital letter T in a circle. There are four train lines, sometimes called the subway. The MBTA also operates the bus system, commuter trains and some commuter boats.

One of the first things you should do is familiarize yourself with an MBTA map that shows all the bus and T routes. Most of the large sta-tions have free bus schedules as well as T maps for sale. For travel infor-mation call 722-3200. The web site is www.mbta.com.

There are four rapid transit train lines that service the Boston area. They all intersect downtown and you can transfer between the lines where they intersect with each other for no extra charge. The lines are known by their colors: Blue, Green, Orange, Red.

Each of the lines is above ground for part of its route, but the Green line is above ground for most of its route. The Green line trains are much different than the others — they look like street cars. The Green line also has four different routes that split off at Copley: the "E" trains run to Heath Street, the "B" trains run to Boston College, the "C" trains run to Cleveland Circle and the "D" trains run to Riverside.

When you first begin riding the T you have to remember just two things in order to get on the right train: inbound and outbound. Inbound always means going toward downtown Boston (no matter which direction that might be) and outbound always means going away from downtown Boston (no matter what direction that might be).

The T is open from 5:00 a.m. to 1:00 a.m. Monthly passes are available.

COMMUTER RAIL

The commuter rail is shown in purple on MBTA maps which is how it got its other name: the Purple line. The commuter rail runs from downtown Boston to the suburbs — in some cases as far as 60 miles away. Fares are slightly more expensive than the T with a maximum fare of around $4.75. Trains leave from either North or South Stations and do not run 24 hours, with the last ride usually leaving the station around midnight.

THE BUS

The MBTA runs 162 bus routes. Most of them are "feeder service" routes that link neighborhoods to train stations. Very few MBTA buses actually service downtown. The ones that you will see in downtown are usually express buses from the suburbs. Bus stops are marked by signs with the "T" logo. Monthly passes are available.

COMMUTER FERRIES

A ferry from Hingham to Rows Wharf sails Monday through Friday. The Navy Yard Water Shuttle sails from Long Wharf to the Charlestown Navy Yard daily.

IMPORTANT MBTA PHONE NUMBERS

- Travel Information Line, 722-3200 or 222-5000
- Customer Relations (i.e. complaints), 222-5215
- Monthly Pass Program, 722-5218
- Transportation Access The Ride, 222-5123; TDD 722-5415
- Lift Bus Info & Reservations, 800-LIFT-BUS
- MBTA Police, 222-1212

FERRIES AND HARBOR CRUISES

Water transportation is definitely an option for many metro Boston inhabitants. Ferries go to downtown Boston from South Boston, Chelsea, Charlestown, Hingham, Hull and Quincy. The Airport Water Shuttle sure beats the Callahan/Sumner tunnels as a way to get to Logan Airport. And in the summer there are boats to the harbor islands, Gloucester, Nantasket and Provincetown. You'll also need a ferry to get to Martha's Vineyard or Nantucket from Hyannis and Woods Hole on Cape Cod.

- **A.C. Cruises**, 261-6633
- **Airport Water Shuttle**, 330-8680
- **Boston Harbor Commuter**, 740-1253
- **Boston Harbor Cruises**, 227-4321

- **Cape Island Express**, 508-997-1688 (Ferry to Martha's Vineyard)
- **Cuttyhunk Boat**, 508-992-1432 (leaves from both New Bedford and Cuttyhunk)
- **Harbor Islands Water Taxi**, 740-1605
- **Hy-Line**, 508-778-2600
- **Massachusetts Bay Line**, 542-8000
- **Steamship Authority**
  Hyannis, 508-771-4000
  Woods Hole, 508-548-3788

TAXIS

You'll find taxi stands all over the city and you can also call for a cab. If you phone, check the Yellow Pages to make sure you find a company that services your neighborhood.

Boston taxicabs are regulated through the **Hackney Carriage Office, Boston Police Department**, 154 Berkeley Street, Boston, 343-4475. For towns outside of Boston, check with your town or city hall for regulations.

LOGAN INTERNATIONAL AIRPORT

As the fish swims, Logan is only two miles away from downtown Boston. However, during those times that you're stuck in the Callahan Tunnel it might as well be 200 miles. If you absolutely must drive to the airport, good luck. Here's hoping that you don't do it during rush hour, Sunday afternoons or holidays. However, you do have other options.

The **Blue Line** goes to **Airport Station** where you can ride a free shuttle bus to the airport. Make sure you read the signs and check your bus because there are three separate shuttles that service different terminals.

The **Airport Water Shuttle leaves from Rowes Wharf** and lands at the airport ferry dock where you can catch a free shuttle bus. The water shuttle runs every fifteen minutes on weekdays and every half hour on weekends and holidays. Call 330-8680 for information.

You can always take a taxi or one of the bus or limo services. There are a number of such services that make regularly scheduled runs to the airport:

- **Bonanza**, 720-4110
- **Concord Trailways**, 800-639-3317

- **Logan Express,** 800-235-6426
- **M&L Transportation,** 938-8646
- **Mass Limousine,** 262-4662
- **Peter Pan Trailways,** 800-343-9999
- **Plymouth & Brockton,** 508-746-0378

AMTRAK

You can catch Amtrak at one of three metro Boston stations: **Back Bay** (145 Dartmouth Street, Boston), **South Station** (Atlantic Avenue) or **Route 128**. Call 800-872-7245 for information.

NATIONAL AND REGIONAL BUS SERVICES

- **Bonanza,** 720-4110
- **Concord Trailways,** 800-639-3317
- **Greyhound,** 800-231-2222
- **Peter Pan Trailways,** 800-343-9999

ONE FINAL NOTE:

If you plan to live in Boston without a car, and many people do, you should purchase a copy of *Car-Free Boston*, a publication produced by the Association for Public Transportation, 482-0282. It's terrifically useful and should be available at most bookstores.

I f you haven't found your new home but you've already moved to Boston, this section is for you. You do have options — short-term rentals of furnished places, YMCAs and YWCAs, youth hostels and, of course, hotels. Most Boston area colleges and universities, however, do not rent out housing to non-students during the summer.

INEXPENSIVE LODGINGS

- **The Farrington Inn**, Brighton, 787-1860 or 800-767-5337, $60-150 per night; they sometimes take a percentage off for longer stays
- **Home Suites Inn**, 455 Totten Pond Road, Waltham, 800-424-4021, $115 per night.
- **Best Western Terrace Motor Lodge**, 1650 Commonwealth Avenue, Brighton, 566-6260, $95-119 per night.

The rates listed above are winter rates. Some hotels raise their rates from May to September so you should call to double check.

MIDDLE-RANGE LODGINGS

- **Holiday Inn Government Center**, 5 Blossom Street, 742-7630. Room prices range from $129-$249, depending on the time of year.
- **Sheraton Boston Hotel & Towers**, 39 Dalton Street, 236-2000. Room prices range from $99 to $219, depending on the time of year and availability. Ask about weekend specials.
- **Westin Hotel Copley Place**, 10 Huntington Avenue, 262-9600. $149 to $265, junior suites $305. Ask about weekend packages, when rooms run prices begin at $169 a night.

[handwritten margin notes: "Commonwealth", "$575", "A Hostely", "Int.", "Fenway", "Bu parking", "267", "$99", "$105", "Kenmore"]

LUXURY LODGINGS

- **Four Seasons Hotel**, 200 Boylston Street, 338-4400. Room prices range from $455 to $610 depending on whether there's a view of the city or the Public Garden. Ask about weekend specials, when rates run around $350.
- **Ritz-Carlton**, 15 Arlington Street, 536-5700. Rates on standard rooms range from $265 to $385, while suites range from $395 to $695. Ask about any promotions.

HOSTELS

- **Boston International Hostel**, 536-9455. If you are a member of the American Youth Hostel Association, you can stay here for $19 a night. Without a membership card you have to pay a whopping $22 per night.

SHORT-TERM LEASES

- **Buckingham Residencies**, 240 Commonwealth Avenue, Boston, 536-5510. Apartments are furnished, utilities are paid, with light housekeeping. Studios run from $600 to $750 per week. One bedrooms from $750 to $850 per week.
- **Bed & Breakfast Agency of Boston**, 720-3540 and 800-248-9262. Rooms ranges from $70-140 per night. Furnished studios and condos are also available on a monthly basis.
- **Boston Short-Term Rentals, Inc.**, 262-3100. Efficiencies, one and two bedroom apartments fully furnished with kitchens. Utilities and local phone included, maid service available. Efficiencies range from $450-$650 per week. One bedrooms range from $500-$800 per week. Two bedrooms range from $700-$1,200 per week. There's usually a discount for a month commitment. Agency fees may apply.

CORPORATE HOUSING

For corporate housing options, contact **Boston Realty Associates**, which deals with upscale apartment buildings in some of Boston's best neighborhoods. Monthly rates range from $1,000 to $2,000 for a studio, $1,500 to $2,800 for a one-bedroom, and up to $3,500 for a two-bedroom.

- **Oakwood Corporate Housing** also has options for Boston, 800-888-0808 or at their web site: www.oakwood.com.

YMCAS AND YWCAS

- **Constitution Inn at the Armed Services YMCA**, 150 Second Avenue, Charlestown Navy Yard, 241-8400. Rooms with two twin beds $59/night. Rooms with twin beds and a kitchen are $69/night. Rooms on the sixth floor, with skylight and kitchen, $79.
- **YMCA, Central Branch**, 316 Huntington, 536-7800. A room for one costs $38/night, breakfast included. A room for two costs $56/night, breakfast included. Available only June to September.
- **YWCA Boston**, 40 Berkeley Street, Boston, 482-8850. $42/night for a single; $64/night for a double. Breakfast is included. Women only.

Rita
→ 2 double
$~~ 110.
(72hrs)

I n Boston, there are so many events taking place that you'll never find the time to enjoy them all, from First Night and the St. Patrick's Day Parade to the Boston Marathon on Patriots' Day. *The Boston Globe's Calendar* section, *Boston Magazine* and *The Phoenix* are among the publications to check for specific dates and details. Also contact the Greater Boston Convention & Visitors Bureau's Travel Planner at 536-4100 or on the web at www.bostonusa.com/index.shtml.

JANUARY

- Martin Luther King Jr. Birthday Celebration
- Boston & Cambridge Hotels Host Food, Wine and Arts Festivals through April

FEBRUARY

- Boston Wine Festival
- Anthony Spinazzola Gala
- Chinese New Year

MARCH

- St. Patrick's Day Parade
- New England Spring Flower Show

APRIL

- The Big Apple Circus
- Swan Boats Return to Public Garden
- Boston Marathon

- Patriots' Day Parade
- Red Sox baseball season opens

MAY

- Boston Kite Festival
- Art Newbury Street
- Memorial Day Activities
- Street Performers Festival

JUNE

- Boston Globe Jazz Festival
- Harborlights Pavilion
- Boston Dairy Festival/Scooper Bowl

JULY

- Cambridge Summer Music Series
- Harborfest
- North End Festivals
- Boston Pops Concert & Fireworks
- Chowderfest
- Bastille Day Celebration
- Puerto Rican Festival

AUGUST

- Caribbean Carnival
- August Moon Festival

SEPTEMBER

- Cambridge River Festival
- Art Newbury Street
- Patriots season opens

OCTOBER

- Harvest Moon Festival
- Columbus Day Parade
- Harvard Square Oktoberfest
- Ringling Brothers Barnum & Bailey Circus
- Tufts 10K Race for Women
- Head of the Charles regatta
- Bruins season opens
- Boston International Festival

NOVEMBER

- Veteran's Day Parade
- Celtics season opens

DECEMBER

- Christmas Tree Lightings
- First Night

All phone numbers are in the 617 area code unless otherwise indicated.

AMBULANCE

Boston 911
Arlington 781-643-4003
Belmont 484-1300
Brookline 911
Cambridge 911
Medford 911
Newton 911
Quincy 911
Somerville 623-1500
Waltham 781-893-1212
Watertown 911

ANIMALS

Animal Bites 911
MSPCA 522-7400
Angell Memorial Animal Hospital 522-6005

BIRTH CERTIFICATES

Suffolk County 727-7388

BOSTON CITY GOVERNMENT

Boston City Hall 635-4000
Boston Mayor's Office 635-4450

Boston Assessor 635-4287
Boston City Clerk   635-4600
Boston Redevelopment Authority 722-4300

CHILD ABUSE AND NEGLECT

Hotline 800-792-5200
Mass. Society for the Prevention of Cruelty to Children . . 587-1500
Parental Stress Line 800-632-8188

CONSUMER COMPLAINTS AND SERVICES

Council of Better Business Bureaus (CBBB) 426-9000
MassPIRG (Mass. Public Interest Research Group) 292-4800
Massachusetts Bar Association, Tel-Law 542-9069
WBZ Call for Action 787-7070
Mass. Exec. Office of Consumer Affairs
     & Business Regulation 727-7780
Division of Registration Investigation Unit 727-7406
Consumer Protection Division,
Office of the Attorney General 727-8400
Mass. Board of Bar Overseers 357-1860
Federal Trade Commission 424-5960
Consumer Product Safety Commission 565-7730

CRISIS HOTLINES

Alcoholics Anonymous 426-9444
Alcohol and Drug Hotline 445-1500
Cocaine Abuse Helpline and Treatment 800-374-2800
Gamblers Anonymous 338-6020
See the White Pages for other crisis hotline numbers

DENTAL EMERGENCY SERVICE

Dentist Information Service, referrals 536-7720

ELECTED OFFICIALS

Boston Mayor's Office 635-4000

Governor's Office 727-3600

FIRE EMERGENCY

Boston 911
Arlington 781-643-4003
Belmont 484-1300
Brookline 911
Cambridge 876-5800
Medford. 911
Newton 911
Quincy 911
Somerville 623-1500
Waltham 781-893-4100
Watertown 911

HOUSING

Building Problems - Boston 635-5300
Discrimination Complaints 565-5308
Public Housing Questions 565-5256

RENT CONTROL
Boston. 635-4200
Brookline. 730-2040
Cambridge 349-6161

LIBRARIES (MAIN NUMBERS)

Boston. 536-5400
Arlington 781-641-5490
Belmont 489-2000
Brookline. 730-2369
Cambridge 349-4040
Medford. 781-395-7950
Newton. 552-7145
Quincy 376-1300

Somerville 623-5000
Waltham 893-1750
Watertown 972-6431

MARRIAGE LICENSES

Boston. 635-4179

MASSACHUSETTS

Office of tourism and travel. 727-3201
Secretary of State's, Citizens Information Service. . . . 727-7030

POLICE

BOSTON
Emergency 911
Business. 343-4200

ARLINGTON
Emergency 643-1212
Business. 646-1000

BELMONT
Emergency. 781-484-1212
Business 781-484-1215

BROOKLINE
Emergency 911
Business. 730-2222

CAMBRIDGE
Emergency 911
Business. 349-3300

MEDFORD
Emergency 911
Business 781-391-6404

NEWTON
    Emergency 911
    Business. 552-7240

QUINCY
    Emergency 911
    Business. 479-1212

SOMERVILLE
    Emergency 625-1212
    Business. 625-1600

WALTHAM
    Emergency 781-893-1212
    Business 781-893-3700

WATERTOWN
    Emergency 911
    Business. 972-6500

MBTA POLICE
    Emergency 722-5151
    MDC Police. 523-1212
    State Police 566-4500
    U.S. Coast Guard. 565-9200
    U.S. Marshall. 223-9721

RAPE CRISIS SERVICES

    Boston Area Rape Crisis Center 492-7273

ROAD CONDITION INFORMATION

    800-828-9104

SPORTS

    Boston Bruins. 227-3200/3206
    Boston Celtics 523-6050

Boston College 552-3000
Boston Red Sox 267-8661
Boston University.............................. 353-3838
Harvard....................................... 495-2211
New England Patriots..................... 800-543-1776
Northeastern College 373-4700
Tufts... 781-628-5000
UMass/Boston 287-7800

STREET MAINTENANCE

Boston.. 635-4948
Arlington 781-646-1000
Belmont 489-8210
Brookline..................................... 730-2177
Cambridge 349-4800
Newton.. 552-7175
Somerville 625-0300
Waltham 781-893-5710
Watertown 972-6420
State 973-7500

TAXES

BOSTON
Excise Tax Info................................ 635-4133
Real Estate.................................... 635-4120
Water & Sewer 261-4848

CAMBRIDGE
City.. 349-4220

SOMERVILLE
City 625-6600
Federal
Income.. 523-1040
Forms...................................... 800-424-3676
State
Income 727-4545
Taxpayers Assistance 727-4545

Refunds. 727-4471
Estate 727-4448

TAXIS

Boston Cab Association 262-2227
Checker Cab Co. 497-9000
Checker Taxi Co. 536-7000
Green Cab and Yellow Cab Association . . 628-0600 & 625-5000
Red & White Cab 742-9090
Red Cab 734-5000
Independent Taxi Operators Association 536-4400

TIME

637-1234

TRANSPORTATION

Logan Airport 567-5400
Amtrak. 800-872-7245
MBTA (route and schedule info) 722-3200

WEATHER

936-1234

ZIP CODE INFORMATION

654-5767

MARIETTA HITZEMAN and her husband moved to Boston in 1991 from Katonah, New York. Originally from Wisconsin, her writing career has included working in political and corporate public relations, news radio and science writing. Currently, she works as a technical writer in Boston.

ED GOLDEN lives north of Boston with his wife, author and travel writer Fran Golden, and their two children, Erin and Eli. Ed grew up in South Bend, Indiana, and headed East after graduating from Indiana University in the early 1970s. He has worked as a broadcast and print journalist with The Associated Press, in high tech publishing and currently in high tech public relations.

READER RESPONSE FORM

We would appreciate your comments regarding the *Newcomer's Handbook® for Boston*. If you've found any mistakes or omissions or if you would just like to express your opinion about the guide, please let us know. We will consider any suggestions in our next edition, and if we use your comments, we'll send you a *free* copy of our next edition. Send this response form to:

Reader Response Department
First Books, Inc.
P.O. Box 578147
Chicago, IL 60657

Comments:

_____

_____

_____

_____

_____

_____

_____

_____

_____

_____

Name: _____

Address _____

_____

_____

Telephone ( )_____

P.O. Box 578147
Chicago, IL 60657
(773) 276-5911
www.firstbooks.com

NEWCOMER'S HANDBOOK
ORDER FORM ®

THE ORIGINAL, ALWAYS UPDATED, ABSOLUTELY INVALUABLE GUIDES FOR PEOPLE MOVING TO A CITY!

Find out about neigborhoods, apartment and house hunting, money matters, deposits/leases, getting settled, helpful services, shopping for the home, places of worship, cultural life, sports/recreation, vounteering, green space, transportation, temporary lodgings and useful telephone numbers!

	# COPIES		TOTAL
Newcomer's Handbook® for Atlanta	_____	x $13.95	$_____
Newcomer's Handbook® for Boston	_____	x $14.95	$_____
Newcomer's Handbook® for Chicago	_____	x $14.95	$_____
Newcomer's Handbook® for Los Angeles	_____	x $13.95	$_____
Newcomer's Handbook® for Minneapolis-St. Paul	_____	x $14.95	$_____
Newcomer's Handbook® for New York City	_____	x $17.95	$_____
Newcomer's Handbook® for San Francisco	_____	x $13.95	$_____
Newcomer's Handbook® for Seattle	_____	x $14.95	$_____
Newcomer's Handbook® for Washington D.C.	_____	x $13.95	$_____
		SUBTOTAL	$_____
	TAX (*IL residents add 8.75% sales tax*)		$_____
	POSTAGE & HANDLING (*$5.00 first book, $.85 each add'l*)		$_____
		TOTAL	$_____

SHIP TO:

Name _____

Title _____

Company _____

Address _____

City _____ State _____ Zip _____

Phone Number ( ) _____

FIRST BOOKS

Send this order form and a check or money order payable to:
First Books, Inc.

First Books, Inc., Mail Order Department
P.O. Box 578147, Chicago, IL 60657
773-276-5911

Allow 2 weeks for delivery